House
by the
Bo Tree

House by the Bo Tree

Ruth Seamands

WORD BOOKS

WACO, TEXAS   LONDON, ENGLAND

HOUSE BY THE BO TREE

Library of Congress Catalog Card number: 69-20231

Printed in the United States of America

To our
four wonderful daughters
Sylvia, Sheila, Sandra, Linda,
who kept us young in our
House by the Bo Tree

Foreword

To write a Foreword for this book is a pleasure as I sit in a hotel room in Argentina between services. With two or three days notice the large church is filled every night with eager seekers, most all highly intelligent.

I've read some chapters of Ruth Seamands' manuscript "House By The Bo Tree" and have felt the glow of her pages as she describes the mission work carried on by her and her devoted husband in faraway India. For the people who pack my meetings and the village people who pack their camp meetings are driven by the same hunger—a hunger for our Heavenly Father. A few nights ago a finely educated, cultured man said to me at the close of my meeting: "I was shocked to hear you say that the only sickness in humanity is homesickness for God. I was shocked for I believe you are right."

I am not "shocked" at the idea that around the world men are sick with "homesickness for God"—I'm delighted. For that "homesickness" is going to drive men ultimately to the Heavenly Father. I deal with the upper crust, so-called, and the Seamands deal with the simple villagers. But the hunger is the same. And the same Gospel meets the needs of both.

So I welcome these pages from "House By The Bo Tree." They tell of a "Missionary Mama" dealing with her hopes and fears, with her children, with broken noses, with calling a "General" a "Colonel," with snakes and rats and camp meeting crowds and the little things that come into a missionary life, and doing it with a lightness of touch and a gaiety of spirit that is not only refreshing but inspiring.

It is inspiring to peep into a missionary house and see the commonplace become the uncommonplace, the ordinary become the extraordinary, the sordid become the sacred. For through all of this lightness and gaiety runs a deep dedication. For the Seamands are dedicated—it runs through all they do and say and are. So in these pages you see more than you read, you see love at work transforming everything; every common happening is filled with meaning, every common bush aflame with God.

I commend it, for it commends itself.

E. Stanley Jones

January 29, 1968

Preface

A few years ago I wrote an account of our beginnings in India entitled *Missionary Mama*. It is still selling well, and many letters have been received requesting a sequel.

In that volume—written from a mother's point of view and not from the point of view of missionary work as such—one can find accounts of many happenings, from jeeps, snakes, and black magic to devil possession.

In this volume also missionary life is never dull, but punctuated with such things as a broken nose, rats, V.I.P.'s, angels, and birth-practices. Love permeates it all. I hope this will foster an interest in and love for the people of India, who are very close to our hearts. Especially close to us are all our co-workers in the South India Conference of the Methodist Church. May God bless them all.

RUTH SEAMANDS

WILMORE, KENTUCKY
July 1967

Contents

Illustrations

1

House by the Bo Tree

There was a bo tree by our house in India. Many centuries previously, Buddha was enlightened as he sat in the shade of a bo tree; and one day as I sat under mine watching monkeys play and chatter and jump through the branches, I realized what was wrong with my guests.

I had been noticing for some time that all our guests had a common, peculiar malady. They got up in the morning with deep lines etched in their faces, and they straightened their spines in creaking sections. By the time lunch was over, the etched lines were smoothed, and they looked happy and satisfied. I thought for a while they had all gotten out of bed on the wrong side, but it finally penetrated—they had gotten out of the wrong bed.

Sleeping on an American innerspring bed myself, I hadn't given too much thought to our poor guests, who were sleeping on the ancient monstrosity inherited along with our eighty-year-old house. It was supposed to be a bed, but it was more like a cradle. On top of its sagging springs was a thick mattress. I had made the mattress cover, and it had been stuffed with raw cotton, twanged through a stick and a string, supposedly to fluff it up.

The twanger wore a red turban, a white loin cloth, and, on his face, a doctor's mask. Holding the stick with the string in his bare toes, he tweaked the cotton from one pile to another. When he thought he had tweaked and twanged enough, he stuffed my mattress cover and sewed it down with large buttons.

Rev. Yates typified our guests. He had traveled far on rutty roads and was tired when he arrived after supper. He smilingly told me good night, and went to bed in the guest room, lulled to sleep by frogs in the water tank. I am sure he started the night level, but gradually his backside sank lower and lower as the old springs sagged closer and closer to the stone floor. By morning his knees and chin nearly formed a perfect O.

Next morning at breakfast, he looked less than rested, with his etches and spine. But after some of my American scrambled eggs (from Indian chickens) he began to feel better. And after a lunch of roast chicken and dressing, with a scoop of ice cream on apple pie, (a near miracle in India) I could see indecision. Rev. Yates couldn't decide whether to pamper his stomach and stay for another lunch, or to coddle his back and go. Of course, a man's stomach is more important. Stomach won; backside lost.

The day of my enlightenment under the bo tree, I realized my reputation couldn't rest on cooking—I had to do something drastic about those beds. So I called in three coolies, gave them instructions in my faltering Kanarese. They smiled, nodded their turbans, then sat cross-legged on the floor and wove bands of heavy white tape through the flat bed springs, pulling the tape tight.

After prayers with our family and servants, I started the washer (the old-fashioned wringer kind) and dumped in some sheets. The guest room needed redecorating, so I persuaded my book-loving husband to paint a little. Working in the guest room between flips of paint and squeaking springs, J. T. and the three coolies discussed Christian and Hindu religions in the Kanarese language. In India, everyone is interested in talking about religion.

By eleven-thirty I had a big pan of pickles brewing, and the smell of spiced vinegar tickled my allergy and kept me sneezing.

"Mommy, what can I do?" plaintively asked Sandy, my six-year-old daughter.

"Why don't you get busy and work a little?" I asked. "Go and dust your room."

"I don't have enough energy to work, Mommy. It's all I can do to drag myself out and play," she answered, knocking over a quart jar as she lounged against the kitchen table.

"Then drag yourself out of my kitchen!" I sneezed.

She went out and chased the horse.

While I was in the middle of putting the fourth tub of sheets through the wringer, an Indian official's wife came in and asked if I could cut her hair. There was a gusty breeze through the house, so I took her to our bedroom for the shearing. Couldn't have wind-blown hair either in the pickles in the kitchen, or in the fresh paint in the guest room.

About three in the afternoon I trudged across the sun-baked compound to see how my seventy-five Indian boys were faring in the boarding school. Part of my job as a missionary was to see that these boys from the villages were clean and well fed. Their hostel was messy, so after a stern lecture, they began to make the dust fly. Village boys do not understand why Americans are so insistent on cleanliness. A few banana skins, peanut shells, and jack fruit in the middle of their bedroom floor didn't bother them at all.

As soon as I came back to the house, I found a paint brush and tried to help J. T. My hands were glued to the brush when the milk man came and called me. He said he knew it wasn't the last of the month, but would I please give him his pay? He needed money because his buffalo was going to have a calf, or some such reason which I couldn't quite understand. Possibly it was because I didn't know the Marathi language, the only one he spoke. I washed my hands with turpentine (after prying the paint brush out of them), cleaned the turpentine off with some soap which took part of the skin, opened the safe, and gave him his forty rupees.

J. T. said he had had enough of women's work around the house, so he wandered off to write a sermon in the shade of the bo tree.

Yellow walls in the guest room had held me spellbound long enough. I found another brush and varnish can and started dousing varnish on the furniture and doors. The wood had begun to grow long, green beards, due to our rainy, moldy weather. I was varnishing the top of a door and trying to keep varnish out of my hair when the telegraph boy came. I had to pry that brush loose again, clean my hands, and sign the paper. I wished I could just bite the paper I was supposed to sign. Teeth prints are almost as good as finger prints, mine especially, because nobody could duplicate my crooked incisors. Somebody had telegraphed a message wanting me to run an errand to the courthouse for him. Errands are just part of a missionary's day. And I had once thought that a missionary only preached the gospel!

Twilight is short in India, and with the sudden dusk, I was ready to drop into bed. Sandy ambled in. "Tell me a story, Mommy. Something that happened when you were a little girl in America. Nothing ever happens around here."

I was too tired to think back so many years. Memory groped in reverse no further than late that afternoon standing still in shock as two crows fell dead out of the bo tree. I was afraid the irritation of their incessant cawing above J. T.'s head might interfere with the sermon he was trying to produce. I should have known that when a sermon is wrestling with my husband, he notices neither crows nor wife.

But trying to be helpful, and supposing I would only frighten the birds away, I squinted allergic eyes and aimed our pellet rifle at the noise in the tree above J. T. Varnished fingers squeezed the trigger twice, and then I stood dumbfounded as the two crows fell, stone dead, one on each side of J. T.

He arose in absentminded dignity between the suddenly silent racketeers, and stalked away to find a more private bo tree. He needed enlightenment.

I needed sleep.

2

Retrospect

How did it happen that I was living in India in a house by a bo tree? It began in Herrin, a little town in southern Illinois during the depression. Everybody knew about Bloody Herrin, because we were the center of gang wars over mine strikes and bootleg whiskey. My parents were strict churchgoing Methodists, so I was brought up in the church. I made good grades in school, but nothing outstanding because it was more fun to have fun than to study. I was a complete extrovert, and if there were any mischief afoot in my circle of Methodist kids, I was right in the middle of it. I had a million friends, but no money. That didn't bother me because very few people did have any.

When I was nineteen, one Sunday our pastor announced that in June our church was going to sponsor a revival. We were to put up a large tent on the church grounds and call in a visiting evangelist. But what made my ears stand up was the further announcement, "And to furnish music for our two weeks of meetings, we have called a quartet of four young men from Asbury College, in Wilmore, Kentucky."

Four of us girls were always together, and none of us had any serious love affairs in progress at the time, so we put our heads together. We decided that when that quartet arrived, we were each going to choose one—just to flirt with—and that during those two weeks, Herrin was going to rock a little. It had been too quiet too long anyway, ever since the bootleggers were put out of commission. This quartet was going to remember Herrin!

Then we heard some sad news; one of the quartet members was married. That cooled us a bit, and we could visualize Herrin rocking a quarter less, but we said, "Let the best three women win!"

Moments of great anticipation come slowly at nineteen, but at last the Sunday finally dawned. That night at the first meeting of the revival, my three friends and I were seated in the front row of the choir. We weren't going to miss a thing. For a month we had speculated and wondered what the quartet was going to be like.

The choir was separated on the platform so women were on one side and men on the other. Wearing a pink dress with my initial embroidered on it, I was whispering something to Katherine when the magic moment came. The quartet filed in from the back of the tent and came toward the platform. I lifted my eyes and froze, though it was June the twenty-eighth. I was looking straight into the vivid blue eyes of the redheaded basso. My heart did a double handspring trying to furnish enough blood to thaw me, and my first thought was, "That's the man I want to marry!" My own thought shocked me, but I couldn't stop looking at him, and every time my eyes veered in his direction, his eyes were glued to mine. I didn't hear a word of the sermon.

When the quartet sang, I discovered he had a marvelous voice, deep, full and rich—unusual in such a young man. I also discovered freckles on his neck. I'd always hated freckles before. When the quartet sat down, I looked at him again, and his eyes were all for me.

I truly forgot about hooking a boy friend just to flirt with for two weeks. I forgot about rocking Herrin, so completely rocked on my own heels was I. After the service was over, Katie nudged me and whispered, "Come on, let's go meet them!"

I wasn't interested in meeting "them," only "him." I'd never been shy in my whole life, but my knees were knocking together as I tottered over to him. He was waiting for me. "My name is Ruth Childers," I said, putting out my hand, "and we're very glad to have you in our church."

I don't know what I expected J. T. Seamands to say, but I was a little disconcerted when he didn't say a word. He was completely tongue-tied. He simply stood there holding my hand and looking at me. We were on a desert island in a murmuring sea of Methodists. I finally remembered my mother was waiting, so I retrieved my hand and floated—yes, floated—out the back of the tent. Turning around for a last glimpse, I saw J. T. still standing there, dumb, still staring after me. He was paying no attention to the people (including my three friends) who had gone to shake hands with him.

When I got into bed that night and looked out the back window at our coal shed, chicken house and WPA privy, they were all bathed in glory. Odd, I'd never noticed their translucence before.

The next night after the meeting, Clarence, one of our church crowd, told me that J. T., the basso, was interested in getting acquainted with me. "And I'm interested too!" I answered.

"Would you two like to go riding with my girl and me?" Clarence asked.

"I will if he will."

So after the second sermon which I didn't hear, Clarence brought his car, his girl, and J. T. around. I thought it strange that J. T. opened the back door of the car and got in first. I had to climb in behind him and shut the door. The idea flitted across my mind that his manners could be improved.

His tongue untied itself that night, and he told me his father was a missionary in India, and that he, J. T., had been in the United States for only three years. He had finished high school in a boarding school in India.

I realized then that he had come from a culture where it's "men first" and that's why I'd been left to shut my own door. I'd read somewhere that in India men always walk ahead of women—and the women usually come trailing along behind, carrying the luggage. I was glad I had no luggage.

Every night for the next two weeks we had a date after church. Love had come suddenly, and our time was short. He told me he had fallen in love with me the minute he had walked into that tent, and I confessed it was the same with me too.

I had a job in Woolworth's, at the ice cream counter. Clerks weren't supposed to entertain guests while at work, of course, so the only way J. T. could talk to me during the day was to come and buy ice cream. He came three or four times every day, bought cones, stood there and ate them and told me how beautiful I was. I know he consumed more ice cream during those two weeks than anybody else in town did all summer long.

The meeting drew near its close, and J. T. and I were panicky. His quartet was booked to sail at the end of the summer on a round-the-world evangelistic tour, to be gone for a year. It was too much! How could we stand to be apart for a whole year when we'd just found each other? We comforted ourselves by saying that the year would really be a good test of our love. But the prospect was terrifying.

Of course I had been going to church every night, and the sermons had begun to soak in. The evangelist, Rev. Tommy Harper ("There'll be Harpers in heaven," he said), was so sincere, preaching especially to the young people, urging us to dedicate our lives to Christ. The quartet fellows had already done so. But J. T. never preached to me.

One day I took a good long look at myself in the mirror and said to *me*: "Look, Ruth, where are *you* going? What are you going to do with your life? Do you want to stay where you are forever? Look at J. T. and the other quartet fellows; they have completely given themselves to Christ. J. T. could be tremendously popular and make a lot of money with his outstanding voice, but he has chosen to use it for God."

That night, my mind was made up. I went to the altar, prayed and told God I was sorry for all my selfishness and sins, and if He'd accept me, I'd like to do something worthwhile with my life. I didn't know what that might be, but I felt very peaceful.

The meeting closed, the quartet left, but glory still hung low over the outbuildings. Letters fresh from the heart flew by fastest trains to and from points all over the United States. Twice more during the summer we were able to be together.

One of those times was when J. T.'s Pennsylvania Dutch grand-mother invited me to her home for a close scrutiny. J. T. had told her that I was the one. I nearly disgraced myself my first night in her home by falling through the seat of a tiny, delicately up-holstered bedroom chair. Her home—much richer than mine, and even with an inside bathroom—nearly petrified me.

By the end of the summer, when the quartet sailed for England on the first part of their tour, J. T. and I knew we were meant for each other. After all, didn't we hear angels singing when we were together?

Another four months passed, and in January the quartet was in Capetown, South Africa. I was receiving letters from J. T. every time a boat docked from Africa. Foreign airmail was not common then.

One Wednesday evening, I went to prayer meeting at our church. Arriving early, I helped myself to some pamphlets from a table, sat down, and began to read one. I was surprised to see that it was written by E. A. Seamands, J. T.'s father. I don't remember what the pamphlet said, but it was about missionary work in India. Sud-denly, as I was reading, something—a voice—spoke very clearly in my mind, "Ruth, if I call J. T. to go to India as a missionary, would you be willing to go with him?"

Now that was the wildest thing I'd ever heard. What ever made me think of that? I concluded, "My mind is overly influenced by reading about India. Power of suggestion." So I mentally shrugged and kept on reading. Again, an insistent voice, "Ruth, if I call J. T. to go to India as a missionary for Me, would you be willing to go with him?"

No one was sitting near me at the time, so who else but God would be speaking to me? I knew that God used to talk to people in Bible days, but that was centuries ago. He never talked to anybody today. Or did He? I began to pray, "Lord, You know I'd make a hopeless missionary. I'm not trained, I don't have a college education, I've never considered living in another country. Besides, J. T. isn't going to be a missionary, he told me he was going to teach music."

The Voice was insistent, "If I call J. T., will you go with him?"

I felt God would not take a straddle-the-fence attitude for an answer. He wanted a "yes" or "no." Finally, not having any peace of mind, I said, "Lord, I don't understand this at all, but yes, if You call J. T. and he wants me, I'll go." After that, I didn't hear the Voice any more. I finished reading the pamphlets, and sat through prayer meeting.

Then I faced a dilemma. Should I write to J. T. about my encounter with God? If I told him, he might think that I was trying to urge him to become a missionary. So I decided not to write about it. I wrote an ordinary letter (full of love and stuff like that) and went to bed. But the next morning I couldn't bring myself to mail the letter.

In our church there was a wonderful woman, Helen Sullenger, who was an inspiration to all of us young people, and in whom we had utmost confidence. She had often advised us on various problems. The next day I went to her house and told her what had happened at the prayer meeting. I finished by asking, "Helen, should I tell J. T. about this or not? He might think I'm wanting him to become a missionary and take me to India with him—and nothing could be farther from my intentions."

She wisely answered, "By all means tell him. I feel this is really of God, and it concerns your whole life. J. T. will understand."

I tore up the letter I'd written the night before, and wrote another telling J. T. what had happened. I concluded by saying,

> You told me once you were going to be a music teacher. I am not trying to direct your life, but this is simply to let you know that if you should ever want to go to India as a missionary, and if you wanted me to go with you, I will. I love you.
>
> RUTH

Letters by sea mail to South Africa took one month for the journey, so I knew I'd have to wait two months for an answer to this important letter. But in exactly *one month* a special letter from J. T. arrived, written on the same day as the one I had sent. He wrote,

> My Dearest—When I was a high school boy in India, God called me to come back to India after finishing my education, to be a missionary there. At that time I answered the call and told God that I would go back, but when I got to America and saw what a marvelous country it was, my commitment began to slip. I thought I could just as well be a preacher in America in more luxurious surroundings, and by the time I met you, I was not even willing to be a preacher at all. I was still a Christian, but felt I could be a Christian in America just as well as India. After I met you, I was afraid you wouldn't have anything more to do with me if you knew I wanted to go back to India, so I told you I was planning to teach music.
>
> But this morning as I was dressing, God spoke to me. He said, "How long am I going to have to strive with you? I have called you to be my servant in India. Once you were willing, but you have gone back on your promise. What is your final decision?"
>
> My heart was miserable, my life defeated. I had not told you the whole truth. I knelt here in my room in Capetown, weeping, and answered, "Lord, if your will for me is to go to India, then I will go."

Immediately I felt joy return to my heart. But then God went on to say, "What about that girl in southern Illinois? She doesn't know about this call. Suppose she is not willing to go with you, then will you reject my call, marry her, and stay in America? Are you willing to follow Me, even if it means giving up Ruth?"

I was staggered by the alternative that faced me. But I am in dead earnest. I have promised God that I will obey Him whatever the cost. So now I am writing this to you. I must do what the Lord wants me to do. I don't know how you feel, but if you are not willing to go to India with me, then our relationship as sweethearts must cease. I love you, and I hope you will come with me.

Yours forever,
J. T.

By the time I read the last two paragraphs, I could barely see the words for tears. An answer—a marvelous, filled-with-wonder answer, in only one month. This meant that the very same day God spoke to me at church in Herrin, He was speaking to J. T. in Capetown, South Africa. And allowing for the difference in time, it was almost the same hour. Would I ever have any doubt that I was meant for J. T. and he was meant for me? Never.

And I never have.

I went to college, and then our career as missionaries in India began. We were sent to the house by the bo tree, and fell in love with the place and the people.

3

Sorry! It's the Sari

I often wore a sari, that beautiful, flowing Indian dress. Besides being graceful, a sari hides a multitude of figure faults.

One evening we were attending a dinner party at our club, and I was seated alone at a small table waiting for J. T. to join me. An Indian gentleman, a good friend of ours, strolled up.

"Good evening, Mr. Desai," I greeted him. "Won't you sit here and talk to me for a while? J. T. will be coming in a few minutes."

"Yes, thank you. How are you, Ruth?"

"Oh, just fine. I haven't seen you for a long, long time."

"No, you haven't been out for tennis lately, have you?"

"No," I answered. "I've been busy. You look as if you had lost a great deal of weight, Mr. Desai. Have you been dieting?"

"Yes, and I feel one hundred percent better. I've lost twenty pounds."

"Twenty pounds! That *is* dieting. You've lost your stomach!"

He eyed me. "You look as if you had put on weight this last while. Why don't you go on a diet too? It is really quite painless, you know."

"Tell me about your diet," I encouraged.

"Well, I think you would like it. I must say I think you looked better the last time I saw you. You've gained a little too much, you know," he said frankly. "Now, this diet is simply diet plus exercise. First thing in the morning you get up and drink one glass of 'Nimbu Pani.' "

"You mean just plain limeade?" I asked.

"Yes. Then after that you must do half an hour of exercise."

"What kind of exercise?"

"Oh, all kinds—bending, kicking your legs, swiveling your hips—all that. Then the only breakfast you have is one cup of coffee, without sugar."

"I don't like coffee."

"Well, one cup of tea then. Don't overeat for lunch or dinner; just eat a normal amount. But every evening, there must be more exercise. Now I like tennis, because that exercises all the muscles. Really, Ruth, you would feel a lot better if you took off some weight. I can give you moral support. Why don't you come out and play a game of tennis with me tomorrow?"

"Oh, I'm not a good tennis player. That's why I don't play with my husband—or rather, why he won't play with me. I spoil his game."

"I'm not such a good player either, but I just play to run. Keeps me limbered up. If you decide to join me, I'll be glad to play you two sets tomorrow. If you lose a few pounds, I promise you'll feel much better."

"I have no doubt of it," I said. "I always feel better when I lose these extra pounds. It won't take me long to lose them, once I start."

Mrs. Desai had come up in time to hear the last of our conversation, and she firmly took her husband by the arm and led him over to a corner, where she whispered something in his ear. I watched, and grinned at him, as he first looked startled, then incredulous. I got up and walked over to tell him he was forgiven. He saw then, that what his wife had just said was true—even though I wore a sari, anyone could tell I was eight months pregnant.

4

Of Pain and Sorrow and Cashew Nuts and God's Care

God's care for His children is never ending. He said, "Lo, I am with you alway . . ." and we have had occasion to prove this over and over. It seems sometimes as if God has a sense of humor in the way He "goes way out in left field" to help us. He expects us to ask for help—we are His children.

When Sandy was born, I developed an infected hip (from a nonsterile injection) which stubbornly refused to heal. Over a period of two years, I had four operations on that huge infection; operations which seemed to do no good at all. Each time the wound almost healed, but not quite, and for two years I was in pain all the time. I couldn't sit straight, lie on my right side, drive the jeep, walk, or do anything without pain.

I had just come home from the hospital after the second of those operations. The doctor had cut deeply into the abscess, and then instead of sewing it up, had packed it full of gauze to absorb infection. The pain was excruciating. I could barely walk, sitting was practically impossible, and driving our jeep was agony. I was nursing my three-months-old baby at the time.

Into my haze of pain one day a good friend came to stay a few days with me. She was seven months pregnant, and was on her way to Miraj Presbyterian Mission Hospital, a hundred miles to the north, for a checkup, and decided to visit me on the way. She had been there a day or two when she suddenly went into premature labor. I knew getting her to Miraj and to her own doctor was impossible. About a mile from our house, down a very bumpy road, was a small maternity hospital, run by an Indian lady doctor and her husband. I took my friend there.

I could barely creep up into the jeep in my own pain. My husband was out preaching in villages, unreachable, and there was nobody else around who knew how to drive a jeep. Down the bumpy road we went, both of us gasping with every jolt, but I got her safely to the maternity home. Her labor was on in earnest.

I stayed as long as I could with her—until it was time to nurse my baby—then crawled into the jeep for the bumps up the hill.

After nursing my baby, I left her in the care of my servant lady, and went back to the little hospital. It was about 2:30 in the afternoon when I arrived. My friend had given birth to one baby, which was dead, and then they discovered there was a twin, which was born about an hour later while I was with her. The living twin was so tiny and premature I doubted that it could live. There was no incubator to keep the baby in, and no modern facilities to care for it.

My friend was in a state of psychological shock, and I felt I should spend as much time as possible with her. So I stayed until the 6 P.M. feeding time, then bumped back up the hill again—every time the jeep hit a big rock or hole in the road, tears rolled down my cheeks.

Back again to the maternity home after supper, and again up the hill at 10 P.M., down the hill to stay with my friend at 10:30. I was almost in shock myself. At eleven o'clock that night the other tiny baby died. Because I was very much concerned about my friend's mental state, I stayed the night with her. I'd had no rest at all and the throbbing pain increased until my whole right side was a hot, searing, jagged sword.

Early the next morning after I had slowly hoisted myself up into the high jeep seat to go home and feed my baby, I put my head on the steering wheel and cried. "Oh God, *please* send somebody to help me! I can't do all this by myself. I *cannot* go up and down this hill driving this bumpy jeep any more, but I *have to*. Please send somebody to help me!"

I fed my baby, ate a little breakfast, and limped back to the jeep. At 10 A.M. I came back up the hill, then down again. My side was ablaze, and my eyes almost refused to stay open.

About 11:30 that same morning, I was sitting in the room with my friend, trying to keep awake, when I heard someone call in the reception room, "Is there a Mrs. Seamands here?"

It was a strange voice, an American voice. I hobbled out and there was a young man I had never seen before. "I am Mrs. Seamands," I said.

"My name is Norman Waters, Mrs. Seamands, and I am from Salt Lake City. I want to know if I could stay with you for a while."

God certainly does do things up right! That morning when I'd cried for help, if God had answered audibly, "All right, I'll help you. Now, what kind of person would you like for me to send?"—if that had happened, and if I had thought of the most unlikely kind of person I could ever imagine and had said, "Well, it really doesn't matter, but why don't you send me a Mormon from Salt Lake City, and just to be different, why don't you have as his job trying to destroy all the worms in the middle of cashew nuts?"—that would have been about as wild as I could ever have imagined. But, as I said before, God really goes way out in left field to help His children sometimes.

I stood staring at my very definite answer to prayer—a large young man standing solidly on two feet and saying—"I am a Mormon from Salt Lake City. I want to know if I can stay with you for a while. I am in this part of India, giving my missionary service for my church. I'm an entomologist, and I'm trying to help the Indian government get rid of the worms in the middle of cashew nuts."

I was too tired. My eyes didn't focus right, and my brain wasn't working. This was the craziest thing I'd ever heard. "Oh, are there worms in the middle of cashew nuts? I eat cashew nuts all the time."

He grinned, "In almost every one. Do you cook them first?"

"My cook does. Is that so bad? What do they want to get rid of them for? They taste pretty good to me."

He must have seen I was dead on my feet. He knew at once I was stupid. He patiently explained, "Because of the worms in the middle of cashew nuts, the Indian government is losing thousands of rupees every year because the United States won't allow wormy cashew nuts imported. I feel I can help the Indian government lick this problem, because I'm an entomologist and an authority on this particular kind of worm."

At the time I couldn't take it all in. Bugs and worms and cashew nuts and governments—who cared about them? I was a mass of pain, and I needed sleep. Tears were rolling and I said simply, "I asked God only five hours ago to send somebody to help me. Can you drive a jeep?"

"Of course!"

I closed my eyes a moment ("Thank you, God"). "You can stay with me forever if you'll drive me up and down this hill, as long as my friend has to stay here, and . . ." I told him what all the tears were all about.

He stayed several months, he drove, he helped my friend and me through the crisis, and he helped the Indian cashew nut growers with their worms.

Yes, God really goes way out sometimes.

5

Crisis

My fourth baby was nearly due and it was time for me to get to the hospital. Our nearest missionary neighbors were the Presbyterians who have a fine hospital in Miraj, a hundred miles from us. Our third daughter, Sandra had been born there. With the hospital so far away, the last month of waiting must be spent there—no such thing as staying at home until labor starts, then making a dash for the hospital. Not over those roads, and not in a jeep through the monsoons!

We packed up, took Sandy, who was six, and went by train to Miraj. I was happy that J. T. could spend the whole time with me there. He could do so only because it was the monsoon season and he couldn't tour in village areas anyway. He was in the midst of writing a book in the Kanarese language, and he could do that just as well in Miraj as in Belgaum.

We stayed with Dr. and Mrs. Evans, and I tried to make myself useful, and kept busy typing letters and working in the hospital supplies room. Sandy played with another missionary child, and J. T. sat at a table on a veranda sheltered from blowing rain and laboriously wrote his book by hand. So the days of the last month before birth were going slowly by. One day two letters arrived. They were from our two daughters in boarding school, nine hundred miles away from us—one from Sheila, aged 8, and one from Sylvia, 12. I opened Sheila's letter first:

> Kodaikanal Boarding School
> September 9, 1956

Dear Mommy and Daddy:

    I am glad it is almost time for our new baby to come. I hope you are enjoying waiting there in the Miraj hospital. Yesterday I had an accident. I was playing ball and ran into a boy's back and now I have a broken nose. It hurt at first but not now. I look funny with it all lopsided, and when I wiggle it, it squishes. No more news now.

> Love,
> SHEILA

Beginning to be in a state of shock, I opened Sylvia's letter:

> Kodaikanal
> Sept. 9, 1956

Dear Mother and Daddy:

    Yesterday Sheila broke her nose and we had a hard time getting the blood stopped. We finally did, and she says it doesn't hurt any more. At first the doctor and nurse said it was broken, and now they say it isn't. Even as dumb as I am, I *know* it is broken. It is smashed clear over on the side of her face, and when wiggled, you can hear the bones grate together. She looks awful and nobody seems to be doing anything about it.

    When Sheila saw the doctor, he asked if Sheila would go down to Vellore and get her nose set. Sheila was so scared she said, "No, don't bother about it. I always did have a crooked nose." Imagine that! Well, I told the doctor she most certainly did *not*. I personally hope they do send her down to Vellore, for I don't want my sister going through life with a nose squashed side-ways. What shall I do about it? Last week I went out hiking by myself and killed a snake. It isn't going to be the last one I kill, so just prepare yourself. Nothing else has happened this week.   Love,

> SYLVIA

My first thought was that if anything else *had* happened that week, I'd have a heart attack! Then I did the best thing to do under the circumstances—I went into hysterics. I could just see my lovely redheaded Sheila going through life with a nose squashed sideways, and my brave daughter Sylvia being killed by snakes while hiking alone over the Palni mountains.

When the doctor calmed me down I said, "J. T., you've got to get Sheila down off that mountain and into the Vellore hospital. Go get her and stay with her. If the baby comes before you get back, well, I'm in good hands here." I mopped tears, and the baby kicked me for such disturbing behavior. "And give Sylvia a good paddling for going hiking and killing snakes alone. She knows very well that's against the rules."

J. T. rushed out to get his suitcase, bedding roll, and water jug ready for the long trip. I sat weeping and mumbling to myself, "And just to think, it has taken that letter five days to reach us. No telling what condition that lopsided nose is in now!"

It took J. T. thirty-three hours to reach Vellore, but he arrived shortly before Sheila, so he was with her the whole time. The school had sent a woman servant with Sheila down to the Vellore Hospital. The doctor took one look at Sheila and rushed her onto the operating table. The break was 7 days old and broken in two places.

After a week of breathing through her mouth while her nose was stuffed and taped, when the bandages were removed, Sheila heard the sad words, "The nose is not straight; we have to do it over."

She suffered through another operation and another healing period before getting an O.K. from the doctor to go back to school.

J. T. kept me informed back in Miraj through telegrams. At first I thought all the upset would cause an early birth, but after the fuss our baby obligingly settled down again and waited for her father's return to Miraj. So he was there and one of the first to welcome her into the world. Another fat, beautiful redheaded girl. We had a Sylvia, Sheila, and a Sandra, but we couldn't agree on another name beginning with "S." So we compromised and named her Linda. Four girls! The thought of all the dowrys staggered us!

6

Villages

J. T. spent a great deal of his time in villages, visiting Christians, witnessing to people who had never heard of Christ; helping poor villages with their problems of schooling, marriage, rights of untouchables, counseling with village pastors, etc. Sometimes he met opposition which wasn't very easy to take.

During our last term in Belgaum, he began to visit a small village which was completely Hindu—not a single Christian family. Most of the people had never seen a white man before, and they called him "kempu-mukha" which means "the red-faced-one." That is the customary village term for Americans, or fair Europeans. He first called on the headman and received permission to speak in the village square. Then he began to play his accordion and sing gospel songs in Kanarese, and in this way drew a crowd. The people were curious to see who knew their language so well that he could sing in it. Then he preached to them.

Most of the people were friendly, but after a few visits, he noticed a coldness among some of the young men. Once while he was preaching in company with two or three Indian preachers, some of the young men of the village began to berate him. They told the people, "Don't pay any attention to this red-faced foreigner. He is only here to trick us. He is up to no good." One of them went on with a long barrage of words against J. T., and wound up by threatening him. Then he and some of the others threw cow dung on J. T. as a sign of distaste and disgrace. Through it all, J. T. stood calmly and told them that he was up to no tricks, he only wanted to tell them of his God and a better way of life.

The next day he wrote a letter to his Dad in which he mentioned that some village people had thrown cow dung on him. Dad Seamands, veteran of thirty years in India, wrote in sympathy. "Don't worry, Son. That's just good fertilizer for the gospel!"

J. T. kept going back to the village and slowly made friends. In the village was one old lady who at first was afraid of J. T., but became friendly, and always talked to him. One day she walked a great distance to visit us in Belgaum. When she reached our house, she was very hot and tired. I invited her in, and she asked for a glass of water. I gave her a full glass. She drank part of it but didn't want it all. She was afraid it would be rude to hand part of the water back to me in the glass, so she glanced around and then just threw the rest of it over her shoulder onto my living room rug. I tried not to gasp. That's the way she would have done in her village home.

She had come in to ask me to take her to the hospital to see about her leg, which was swollen and full of pus. I first took her to the government hospital, and waited with her for a long time until she could see the doctor. The doctor said I had brought the lady to the wrong place, and told me where to take her.

"But that's the leprosy hospital!" I exclaimed.

"Yes, she has a type of leprosy."

I was nervous about the whole thing, but drove her way out in the country to the leprosy hospital. The doctor there examined her, treated the sores and gave her some medicine. He told me not to worry; this type of leprosy was not very contagious. I was relieved. Several times this old lady came to our house, walking about ten miles each time, and I took her back to the leprosy hospital for treatment. I think it gave her prestige in the village to be able to say she had visited us. She loved to come into our house, look around, and touch things, and ask me about the furniture, especially in the kitchen. My kitchen had a wood-burning stove, no built-in cupboards, two marble-topped tables for working area, and a rough stone floor. But it was beautiful compared to hers, where there were three stones put together for a fireplace, and no pipe or even a window for the smoke to go out. She used to look at my stove, with the fire and smoke controlled, and shake her head in disbelief. When I showed her the reservoir at the back of the stove which always contained hot water, she was amazed.

She wanted to be kind to me and always brought a present of some foodstuffs she had made. It was usually like vermicelli, a kind of very thin spaghetti. She said she made it in her house.

Outwardly, she never became a Christian, but in her heart, I think she is a believer in Christ. She is a widow, and as such has no standing in her Hindu community, for widows are looked down upon. So if she openly confessed Christ, she would be forced out of her community and have no place to go.

Somehow, I have a special feeling about this woman. Whenever I would go to that village with J. T., she was always one of the first to greet us. She invited us to her house and gave us tea. Village people are very hospitable, and if they had nothing to offer us, sometimes they would go to a neighbor's house and borrow some milk, boil it and give it to us.

In one village lives an elderly man whose name is Oomana, a Jain by religion. Jains are the strictest of Hindus—vegetarians, not eating any kind of meat, fish, nor even eggs. They have a horror of taking any kind of life. It used to be that Jains would wear a veil over their faces to keep from inhaling and killing any germs in the air, and they used to sweep the path ahead of themselves as they walked to keep from stepping on and killing any kind of insect.

Several times Oomana had heard J. T. preach the Christian

message in his village, and on a few occasions had invited J. T. into his home in order to ask him questions about Christ. When God answered J. T.'s prayer for a baby for a childless couple, like everyone else in the village, Oomana heard about it.

Oomana knew there was a cobra around his house. He had seen it several times but was unable to catch it. He did not want to kill it; he simply wanted to take it back to the jungle. So he made a kind of trap with string and fishhooks. He caught two frogs and impaled them on the fishhooks. Cobras like frogs, so he hoped the cobra would swallow a frog and thus be caught on a hook. But the trap failed, and the cobra was not caught.

One night, Oomana was sleeping in his small mud hut in his village, when suddenly the big cobra fell down from the rafter onto his face and bit him on the forehead between the eyes. At his cry of pain, Oomana's wife came running. When she found what had happened, she began screaming, and the whole family rushed in. They all began to mourn and cry, knowing that Oomana would soon be dead.

Then Oomana remembered hearing J. T. preach of Christ who had healed people when He was here on earth, who had opened deaf ears and blind eyes, and, yes, even raised a man from the dead. He remembered, too, the quarrel he had had that very afternoon with his nephew. The thought came to him then that if he died, his nephew might be accused of poisoning him. Though they had quarreled, he did not wish that to happen.

He was becoming dizzy, his vision was cloudy. He was seeing two of everything. He decided to do what he could, and then pray to this new God of the missionary.

There was no doctor nor nurse in the village. The only kind of germ-killer Oomana had in his village hut was some permanganate crystals. He asked his wife to bring him the sharp knife, and he made a cut in his forehead where the cobra had bitten him. Then he poured some of the permanganate crystals into the wound. He

Oomana and J. T.
God healed
Oomana from a
cobra bite.

lay back on his string cot and prayed, "Oh Lord Jesus, if you are the true God, save me now from this death." He told his wife and family to leave him alone and to stop their mourning. His faith must have been very great. Then he sank into sleep.

His wife sat beside him all night, expecting to see him die any minute. Usually, one bitten by a cobra is dead within thirty minutes; at least within an hour. But Oomana did not die. It was a miracle that the next morning he was still alive.

He told everyone in the village that Jesus had delivered him from the bite of the cobra, just as He had answered the prayer for the baby boy.

A few days after the cobra incident, Oomana sent a message asking J. T. to visit him. J. T. was amazed when he heard this story. As a thanksgiving offering, Oomana gave J. T. four rupees to help someone else hear about Christ. He also gave J. T. the snake trap, which we still have.

When I first heard the story, like Thomas, I doubted a little. Being a practical person, I wondered whether to give credit to the Lord or to the permanganate. But I checked with a doctor friend. He said that permanganate crystals will kill germs, but would not be strong enough to nullify cobra venom. He said perhaps the fact that Oomana cut himself had allowed some of the poison to drain off, but that would not have saved him either. So, I had to be convinced; the Lord must have saved him.

Oomana has never taken Christian baptism, for fear of persecution. In his heart he truly believes in Christ. Some time later when the Jains were taking up a collection in the village to build a new Jain temple, he refused to give anything toward it. For this, and for his Christian belief, he suffered threats and persecution. But he stood firm in his belief in Christ. He was alive, and he knew that was a miracle.

Some time afterward an Indian Christian lady doctor, Dr. Maria Salvanayagam, and two Christian nurses started a dispensary in Oomana's village. For the first time, the people there had medical care. Then the people asked the mission to send them a teacher to start a school in the village. More people were converted, and now there is a thriving church there.

One of the new converts was Oomana's son. After his conversion he came into Belgaum, and attended our mission high school. A year later, he married one of the village nurses who was helping Dr. Salvanayagam. The young couple then went to Bangalore where Oomana's son was employed in a print shop.

All went well for a time, but then Oomana's son's Christianity began to slip. He fell in love with a Hindu woman, and a short time later his young Christian wife died under extremely suspicious circumstances. Then the man married the Hindu girl, and the last report we had of him was that he had again been drawn into Hindu circles.

These things have grieved Oomana. He is still our friend. When J. T. and I visit villages now in the Belgaum area, all doors are open to us. The Christian message is welcomed there. Each patient who visits the dispensary hears about Jesus, and the children hear about Him in their school. We were happy to be co-laborers with Christ in such a venture.

7

Progress

Independent India is now twenty years old. We were there in 1947 when the Indian constitution was signed, and in 1948 when Gandhi was shot. We, like most others, were stunned by the awful civil war which followed. In 1957 we helped celebrate India's tenth birthday. The day is called Republic Day, and is always celebrated by parades, headed by military bands playing Jana Gana Mana, the national anthem, and proudly holding aloft the tricolored flag of orange, green, and white. During the first ten years, India had made rapid strides in a number of ways.

India is a very complex country. Many people think of it in terms of villages and poverty, snakes and elephants and sacred cows, but certainly that is not a complete picture. In between the two extremes of village poverty on the one hand, and riches of a few on the other, there is another class which is rapidly increasing. This is the new middle class of people: teachers, doctors, judges, lawyers, clerks, government officials and employees, merchants, etc.

We lived for many years in close contact with village people; hence, we are very much aware of their joys, sorrows, poverty, superstitions, their lethargy and reluctance to change their mode of life. I feel I know village people a great deal better than do some Indians themselves who have always lived in cities, and who are often not aware or concerned about village people. However, I would not be fair to some millions of Indians if I gave the impression that *all* India is a village. About 75 percent of the people live in villages.

India has an excellent transportation system. You can go by train, plane, or bus just about anywhere. In Belgaum, we were connected by daily plane service to Bombay in the north and Trivandrum in the south. Scores of diesel buses left and arrived at all hours of the day, connecting us with all the towns and villages in the district, and, in addition, at least a dozen passenger trains passed through our city each day.

Education is advancing too. Just during the first ten years of independence, many more thousands of young people were seeking education. Whereas a generation ago the majority of schools were mission or church schools, now the government was taking a most active part in bringing education to all levels of society. In Belgaum new schools were going up all the time. By 1957 we had sixteen high schools, including a technical school; eight colleges, including a law college, teachers training college, commercial college, and regular arts colleges. It was quite a sight to go down the street at school time and see the thousands of students pouring into the schools. At the time of independence, in 1947, there were only seventeen universities in all of India, but by 1957 this figure had more than doubled. Hundreds of applications for entrance into colleges, particularly professional colleges, had to be turned down each year simply because of lack of accommodation. Now with this increase in education has come a new awareness and a refusal on the part of many to accept the old village way of life. More and more people are moving to the cities where opportunities are greater.

The barriers of caste are slowly but steadily breaking down. Formerly only high caste people could enter the temples to worship, but now, with the abolition of caste by constitutional law, members of all castes may enter. The "untouchables" are also allowed in restaurants, and are permitted to draw water from public wells.

With independence and the increase of education has come a greater consciousness of civic duty and responsibility. A good example of this can be seen right in Belgaum. For all the years that Belgaum has been a city (population 110,000), there has been no city water system. Everyone was dependent upon his own compound well, and no one bothered to inaugurate a scheme for piping a continuous water supply into town. Consequently, during the dry season (three months before the monsoon season each year) many people suffered for lack of water. Some had to walk great distances to find a well with water. Almost every year we had to import carts and carts of water for our compound use, because the pump in our own well was just pumping up mud. Now, with the public conscience aroused, people have begun to stir and wake up to their responsibility. Recently the cornerstone for a new reservoir was laid. It would have been great to be able to flush our toilets for all those years in Belgaum without heaving a big bucket of water into them!

The Indian government has inaugurated several five-year-plans, which have done and will do a great deal for Indian life, especially in rural areas. One of the most necessary projects is the construction of dams and reservoirs. Every year in India, at some place or other, disastrous floods occur. In other sections the rains fail and famine conditions prevail. The last two years have seen the latter.

About forty miles from Belgaum, the government has constructed a fine dam, with several long canals, which will bring thousands of acres of dry land under cultivation. Whereas there used to be a minor famine in this area almost every other year, now the entire landscape and economy of the district have been changed.

Community projects now cover almost the entire country. These include a threefold program of agriculture, education, and health. Farmers are being taught better methods of farming, including the use of better seeds and fertilizers and rotation of crops. In each large central village, a new high school is being constructed. Also in many central villages, small dispensaries are being put up.

In cities, one can see not only the dwellings of the poverty-stricken, but also nice homes, well kept. On trains and buses we meet educated, cultured people who are aware of world problems. We have many good friends among this class and have learned to appreciate and love them.

One friend, a doctor, is doing a wonderful job of helping his people. He and his wife, also a doctor, run a clinic and hospital in a small town. They could no doubt get a much better salary in a big city hospital, but they prefer to stay where they feel the need is greater. All their earnings are poured back into the bettering of their hospital. A few years ago, when the doctor felt he needed more experience and training in surgery, his Hindu friends in the town made up a purse of thousands of rupees and sent him, a Christian, to America for a year's study.

Another friend is a high police official, greatly respected for his honesty and integrity. A retired Christian judge is active in our church program. He, together with a Christian banker, interest themselves in finding jobs for boys just graduated from high school. The mechanics who kept our jeep in repair are a family of four brothers who are honest and industrious, and who do not over-charge. They are very much respected in the community. We have friends among Hindu doctors, lawyers, teachers, professors, and merchants with whom we have had many happy hours.

After twenty years of independence, India's problems are certainly not solved, but she's on her way.

8

Gold and House Pests

Our town of Belgaum is close to the border of Goa, and we often heard tales of brisk smuggling from Goa into India. Goa was owned by the Portuguese before it became a part of India. It was a free port, so everything could be bought cheaper there than in India; hence the smuggling. Particularly was gold a smuggling favorite. We heard that police caught people who had padded their clothes with gold, had stuffed it into their noses, or ears, had lined their bullock carts with it, and had hidden it in every conceivable place, just to get it into India.

One day I had to go to the government hospital to have the abscess in my hip dressed. That day while in the operating room having the wound cleaned and dressed, I looked out the window and noticed for the first time a single, small brick-walled room, with only one barred window, and one door with a policeman sitting in front.

"What is that room?" I asked the doctor. "I've never noticed it before."

"You see, police often have prisoners who are ill, and they are cared for in that room," the lady doctor answered.

I said, "That prisoner in there doesn't look very sick. He just keeps walking up and down."

She grinned and shrugged. "Probably has the stomach ache." The doctor continued, "You see, the police were tipped off that that man was smuggling gold into India from Goa. They caught him at the station but couldn't find any gold. So they brought him in here for X-ray this morning. We found twelve pieces of gold in assorted parts of his digestive system."

"So?" I prompted.

"So they put him in that little room, gave him a big dose of castor oil and a pot and a policeman at the door!"

I learned later that it was four days before they recovered the last piece of gold, and hauled the prisoner off to a proper jail. Then the poor policeman was released for more exciting and less odious duties!

Besides my hip wound which lasted for two years, for most of my Belgaum years I had a few other woes. I really didn't know what to do about the pests which were omnipresent in our house. Rats. Rats. Great rats running all over that house every night. They chased each other snickering around my bed, knowing I couldn't sleep. They knocked down cans in the storeroom. Every night they got into my tall flour can on the kitchen table. One night I heard a familiar scratching. I stood in the kitchen door in the bright moonlight and watched a big rat stand on his hind legs and push the lid of the flour can with his nose until the lid clattered onto the floor. In a second the rat was down in the flour. If I could have caught him, I'd have dusted him off, for American flour was so precious, but when I swooped down, he escaped, a white ghost.

I used to be awakened in the middle of the night by rats thumping around in the storeroom. It sounded like a robber invasion. Because of them I had to can everything. My rice, flour, wheat, cheese, everything was in cans; even my nylon stockings and slips. The rats ate all the paper labels off the cans in the storeroom, so I didn't know whether I was opening soup or fruit for dinner. It was always a nice surprise.

One night they had a real wingding. They ate the legs of J. T.'s good nylon suit off about the knees. We nearly collapsed laughing the next time he put that suit on.

Sometimes J. T. used to shut himself in the storeroom with the rats and a hockey stick. He'd been a good hockey player as a boy, and he was still fast. I would hear a flop, smash, thump, crash and bang, and when he opened the door again the floor would be littered with the dead and dying. It looked like a battleground.

Once when Sylvia was home from boarding school she shot a big fat rat which was climbing straight up the storeroom wall. When she shot it, it was halfway up to the ceiling, but slid back down to the floor and raced across Sylvia's bare foot on its way out through the dining room. Sylvia jumped higher than the rat had climbed.

In trying to keep the rats out of the house it did no good at all to shut the doors. The lower corners of every teakwood door in the house had been neatly chewed into half-moons, just big enough to allow the rats to race through. This was their own private tunnel system, allowing them access to every room in the house. They ate holes in all our tents, which we used from year to year in camp meetings. They ate soap in our bathrooms, and toilet paper, which is an expensive luxury item in India. They got into the table drawer of the kitchen and chewed on the handles of knives and ate half my rubber scraper. That was the last American scraper I had, so I got mad and did something about it.

I got a Siamese cat and kept it inside. That cat slunk around at night, and those rats suddenly got quiet as mice. We kept the cat every night in our house by the bo tree, and began to enjoy some nights of unbroken sleep, when we suddenly discovered we were jumping. In fact, the whole place was jumping. Fleas. Fleas! Everywhere! ! We jumped at odd moments, and we scratched in odd spots. Then we shooed the cat out the back door. We squirted DDT everywhere, but the fleas loved it. They still hopped, and we still jumped and scratched. With the cat gone, the rats came back.

I thought I had to make a choice. I didn't know whether to take the rats without cats and without fleas, or to take the cats and fleas without the rats. But it really wasn't my choice. The cat had kittens, new fleas hopped into being by the thousands, the rats had little ratlets, and it was all I could do to keep from having the screaming-meamies.

Having a tame cat and kittens on the doorstep wasn't enough. Wild cats invaded our attic. Several wild cats, or civet cats, came to take the place of the first one we shot. Those civet cats ran and howled and fought all night on the ceiling over our heads. So I had cats on the doorstep, civet cats in the attic, fleas in my bed, rats everywhere, and bats in my belfry.

How I often wished I could read a nice, calm American newspaper!

9

Python and Praise

Camp meeting time rolled around again. We unpacked all our tents, nearly a hundred of them, and hired coolie women to spread them out on the grass over our fourteen-acre compound. Then the women set to work to mend holes caused by rats during the past year of storage. While the women worked, their babies crawled all over the tents, dressed only in shirts and wool caps. Village babies never wear diapers; consequently we often have stinky tents!

With an accumulation of patches acquired over several years, our tents looked as if they had been in the wilderness for forty years. But nobody paid any attention to the holes or patches at camp meeting. We just lived in them and hoped the snakes would stay outside or down by the river.

We heard about an interesting member of our Belgaum community. Once J. T. and I were invited to dinner at the home of an army captain. He was a Christian, and lived across town from us. As we neared his house, we had to cross a small bridge. It was quite dark in that section, but I noticed a small blue light burning under the bridge.

"Why is that blue light burning under the bridge at the side of your house?" I asked, when we entered the Captain's house.

"There is a very large python between fifteen and eighteen feet long which lives under that bridge," the Captain answered. "Some Hindus nearby worship the snake and, of course, fear it. Every night one of them lights the blue light and puts eggs and milk there for the python to eat. He is well fed, never leaves his home under the bridge, so he doesn't eat up any dogs, cats, rabbits, or children."

"You must be scared to death to live so close to that snake all the time. And you don't even have any screens on your house! I wouldn't sleep a wink if I knew a big python was that close to me!"

He laughed, "Aw, I'm not afraid of the snake leaving its place as long as it is well fed. A python is not dangerous unless it is hungry. It sleeps most of the time when well fed, and evidently this one is. We've lived here for two years now, and that blue light has been under the bridge every night since we've been here. That's the sign the snake has been fed."

We had a tasty dinner at the Captain's house, but I kept my feet up on the rung of my chair (as if that would have helped any with a hungry python around!) and I kept looking over my shoulder at the shadowed doorway.

It's always fun to go to camp meeting, set up our tent by the side of the river, and get our camping kitchen in order. J. T. takes out a work detail two days in advance to dig long slit trenches to be used as latrines by the village people. (We have our own little private trench in our own little private latrine tent. I simply couldn't use a community one). When the meetings start, one of the standard announcements at every service is that every person must *be sure* to use the dug-latrines, and help keep the campgrounds clean. With five hundred people on the grounds, if everyone went to the toilet anywhere he wanted to as people often do in villages, living would become rather difficult in a few days.

Many times we have American visitors come to our camp meetings, and of course they cannot understand what is being said, since it is being said in the Kanarese language. I always sit by them to translate. Every time I had to translate the latrine announcement, they usually got so tickled they were almost hysterical, especially with the final instruction, "After doing your job there, rake some dirt into the trench to cover it up!" What an announcement!

One day while J. T. was doggedly digging, with the sweat pouring down his face, I said, "Honey, somebody should award you a Ph.D. of B.L.D., that is, a Ph.D. of Better Latrine Digging."

He wasn't impressed, just wiped the sweat and said, "This is one job they didn't tell me about in the School of Missions. If I ever teach mission classes, I'll teach this. But I'll give it a fancy name to fool them. I'll call it Techniques to Tropical Ministry."

But the physical side of life took second place during camp meeting time. Village Christians came to get their spirits fed and revived. Many came to hear the Gospel for the first time. Many were converted and became Christians in spite of the persecution they knew they would have to face when they went home to their villages.

And not only poor villagers came; many middle class people from the nearby towns came also. There were teachers, lawyers, bankers, businessmen of all kinds. Some came out of curiosity.

J. T. started our camp meeting when we first went to Belgaum many years ago. Dad Seamands, an old hand at jungle camp meetings, came to help us. In our first camp, there were only about twenty people present, and all were mission workers: village teachers and preachers. We want to a desolate spot way out in the jungle, and the only water we could find to use was drawn out of a stinking mud hole. A year later we were able to rent a few acres of land by the Khanapur River. There we had plenty of river water to use, and plenty of firewood. Every year our congregation in the jungle grew.

The singing was spirited and a big part of the meetings, because Indian people like to sing. Many brought their drums, horns, cymbals; and the rest just clapped their hands with the music, and many times they sang all night. Sleeping was a little difficult.

Preaching there is different than in America. Indian people feel they haven't even been preached to if the sermon is less than an hour and a half long; they will sit for a very long time. So the minister preaches for a while, then bursts out in song, and the congregation joins in. Sometimes people get up and stretch and sing a while, then sit down cross-legged on the mats again and the preacher goes on with his next point. Sometimes a sermon lasts three hours. If babies get hungry, mothers nurse them right there. It is their custom, and nobody is embarrassed. Mothers don't want to miss a word. If older children get tired, the mother unrolls some Indian bread from a handkerchief; they eat it, lie down and go to sleep.

Our meetings are under the trees, where a large tent-roof has been put up. The camp "walks" in the month of February in our area, for that is the dry season. Nobody has to worry about getting wet.

This seven-day meeting fulfills a great need for Indian Christians. Living in a country which is so predominantly Hindu, with Hindu customs and holidays being celebrated all the time, Christians must have a substitute. This camp makes them feel that they are not just a small isolated group missing all the fun of religious celebrations.

Many of the songs they liked to sing were those which J. T. had written. They are Indian type songs: Indian tunes, with words in Kanarese, telling some Bible story or bringing home some Christian truth. The Bible speaks of many gifts, but God must have thought up an extra one for J. T. The gift of writing this type of music has done much to further the joy of Christians in this area. Everywhere we used to go, from Christian village to Christian village, we could hear them singing J. T.'s songs. One village used to teach them to another, and thus they go across South India.

Some people have accused the Christian church in India of being built up only from the untouchables and the outcastes. But as Bishop Pickett so aptly put it, "You must not judge Christianity by the type of people who accept it. You must rather judge it by the type of people it produces." And Christ is building His church in India with people from many castes, different walks of life, and also from different religions.

One night at our camp when it was J. T.'s turn to preach, he changed the order of the service. After the singing he said to the audience, "We are in a courtroom tonight. I am going to call to the witness stand four witnesses. I will appoint three judges to bring in a verdict. I am appointing my father, one village preacher, and the third, a village layman, as judges. After they hear all the witnesses, they must bring in a verdict. Now I call the first witness. He is to tell us what Christ has done for him."

The first witness was a simple villager, uneducated, dressed in a dhoti and turban, with a long-tailed shirt hanging down under his coat. He spoke in poor Kanarese, but with great sincerity. He said, "Dear friends, I was born an untouchable in the Hindu religion, but I heard of Christ through this missionary (J. T.). I gave up my idols and put my trust in this Christ. I was an untouchable, but God touched me. I was an outcaste, but God took me in. I was born in lowly circumstances, but God lifted me up and made me His child. Now I am following Him."

When he finished, the whole audience shouted, "Jaya Christ!"

The second witness was called. He was better dressed, spoke in high-class Kanarese, obviously was well educated. He addressed the audience: "My friends, I was born a high caste (Brahmin) in the Hindu religion. I was proud like the Pharisees of the New Testament. I very carefully observed the ceremonies prescribed by my religion, such as a daily bath, the daily worship of the gods, recitation of my sacred scriptures and slokas. I wanted to find peace, but I could not find it in my religion. Then I heard of Christ and accepted Him as my Saviour. He pulled me down from my

self-righteousness, and He humbled me. I used to despise the untouchables, would have nothing to do with them whatever, but now
I can accept them and love them as my brothers. I am now a disciple of Christ."

Another wave of "Jaya Christ" (victory to Christ) from the
congregation.

The third witness was called to the platform. He too was well
dressed. He said, "Friends, I was born a Muslim and followed the
prophet Mohammed. I was very religious. I memorized portions of
the Koran and carefully kept the rules of my religion. I prayed five
times a day and gave alms to the poor. I observed faithfully the
Ramzan fasts—one of our most important occasions. During
Ramzan month, no true Mohammedan will eat or drink anything
during the hours of daylight. We get up at three o'clock in the
morning and cook a big meal and eat. Then nothing else touches
our lips until after dark. We are not even supposed to swallow
saliva. I prayed much, denied myself pleasure with my wife, but
nothing gave me peace in heart and mind.

"Then I began to read the New Testament, and I saw my sins
and I saw my Saviour. When I came to the words of Jesus, 'I am
the way the truth and the life,' I felt my search was at an end. I
saw that Jesus was more than just a prophet like Mohammed. He
was the Redeemer. So I trusted Him and became His disciple. I
was cast out of my home and disinherited by my father, but God
took me into His kingdom and made me His son. I used to despise
these Hindus because they worshiped idols, but now God helps
me to love them."

"Jaya Christ" rose from every throat.

Then J. T. called the fourth witness. He was educated and well
dressed. He began his witness, "Dear friends, I was born a high
caste Hindu, but during my youth I became disgusted with the
old-fashioned ideas and idolatry of my religion. I knew those idols
could not answer prayer. I decided that religion was all useless. I

got in contact with some Communists and was attracted by their promises of a better way of life for our country. So I joined them and became a Communist. But when they started to teach me to lie, to destroy, and even to kill, if need be, for the Communist causes, I began to see that Communism is not the answer to a good way of life. I had no stomach for killing. One day somebody gave me a New Testament and I began to read it carefully. I decided that this is true religion, and that Jesus Christ alone could uplift the world. So I decided to follow Him and I became a Christian. Now I am striving to help establish His Kingdom upon the earth. They say Communism is revolutionary, but Christianity is the world's most revolutionary force!"

After the four men had finished speaking, J. T. then stepped between them, with the former untouchable and high caste on his right, the former Muslim and Communist on his left. Then he said to the audience, "I am a man from the West. The same Christ that these friends found here in India, I found in America. When I put my trust in Him, he changed my life and made me His child. Now I feel that I am a brother to these other four witnesses. We are all one in Christ." Then he put his arms around all four of them and asked the three judges for their verdict.

The three judges went into a huddle while the congregation sang a triumphant Kanarese song. When the song ended, the Indian pastor stepped forward as spokesman for the judges. He said, "Friends in this congregation, having heard the witness of these four, and how Christ has redeemed them, our verdict as judges is that Christ can save men of all castes, creeds, and countries. He can save men from East and West, and He is Saviour of *all* men who believe on Him."

By this time the congregation could not sit still any longer. They stood and, with arms raised high, everybody shouted in unison, "Yesu Masih Maharajah Ki Jai!" ("Victory to Jesus the Messiah!") I doubt if any of them will forget that camp meeting.

10
The V.I.P.'s and I

The most unforgettable character that I met in India was a Hindu woman whom I learned to love very dearly. She introduced herself to me at an exclusive dinner party at the Officers' Club (though I'll never know why I was asked). The elite of the city of Belgaum, both in civilian and military life, were all there, and she should have been talking to them according to her station in life. But she took pity on me, an ordinary foreigner. "I am the Rani of Sawantwadi," she said.

A queen. A real queen, introducing herself to me!

I looked at her obvious wealth: three strands of perfectly-matched pearls, a diamond the size of a frog's egg, and a sari trimmed in gold.

"Come on, let's go eat. I'm starved," she said. A Rani as hungry as I at 10 P.M.

When I got to know her better, I found she was as homelike as a tabby cat, but when displeased with one of her many servants, majestic with scorn. I came to know her so well that our jeep rattled up her elegant drive whenever I pleased. But neither her family nor closest friends could see her any day until she had had her bath and performed her favorite "pujas" (acts of worship) in her own private shrine in her house each morning at 9 o'clock.

She was obsessed with going to movies, and went almost every afternoon. She was short, handsome; she loved good food, was overweight, chewed bright red betel nut, and smoked small cigars which she ordered from Switzerland blended especially to her taste. Her palace was full of servants, but once I found her squatting beside an open fire cooking her own chappatties. I sat down and had some with her, dipping the big brown pieces of bread into the spicy curry juice.

She and I were the only women drivers in Belgaum, and we were always stared at. She raced her sports car through bicycles, bullock carts, donkeys, stray cows and people. I was not quite so jazzy in my ex-World War II jeep.

Though by custom a Hindu widow should not wear jewelry and colors, Rani Sahib regally defied her own religion and always flaunted her jewels and colored saris. Once she went with my husband and me to a studio to have some publicity pictures made. J. T. had borrowed a coat of gold cloth, with a gold turban to match, from her son the Rajah, and was carrying the Rajah's ceremonial sword tied with a wisp of gold chiffon. Rani Sahib thought I should wear more jewelry, so she took off her enormous diamond ring and put it on my finger for the picture. I can imagine the shock our patrons in America got when they saw that picture!

Rani Sahib and I became very close friends. Many times she dropped into my house unannounced, but when I knew she was coming, I always had two of her favorite foods ready—hot, raised, glazed doughnuts and homemade ice cream.

She wanted to teach me how to play mah-jongg, the Chinese gambling game at which she spent many hours with some of her friends. After I'd refused several times, she asked, "Why won't you learn? We could have some good times together."

The last thing in the world I wanted to do was sound pious, but I answered, "Rani Sahib, I don't learn mah-jongg because I don't believe in gambling."

She said, "Phooey, I don't need any money I get from gambling at mah-jongg. If you will play with us, we'll never gamble at it. I have other friends also who won't gamble at it."

I found that mah-jongg is a fascinating game, and though it is the national gambling game of China, one can have a very good time just *playing*.

Rani Sahib put our names up for membership in the Belgaum club and we were voted in. As members of the club, we got to know all the upper class of Belgaum, and were also privileged to meet every celebrity who came to Belgaum. Under Rani Sahib's sponsorship, I felt we were really elevated in the scheme of things.

Everyone was excited when we heard one day that General Shrinagesh, Commander in Chief of all the Armed Forces in India, was coming to Belgaum, and that our club was giving a tea for him. I was appointed to serve on the committee that planned the tea, so was in the receiving line, beside Rani Sahib.

I wore a yellow suit, and must say I looked pretty peppy for an old lady of thirty-nine. At the time the General was due to arrive, all the members were standing on the veranda of the club. We waited for just a few minutes, and in roared two uniformed army policemen on motorcycles, as an escort for the General. The police wore khaki-colored uniforms and steel helmets of the same hue. The receiving line was all in order when the General arrived. I wasn't trying to poke fun at the police, but I was just feeling silly, so I whispered to Rani Sahib that those steel helmets reminded me of baby's pots and would look better with handles. Rani Sahib raised an eyebrow and tried to keep a straight face while she shook hands with the General. I stood, tall in yellow, towering over little Rani Sahib, and tried to keep dignified too while I shook hands with the General.

He wore dark trousers and a white Jodhpur coat instead of his uniform. He was very gracious, shaking hands with us all. He was not as tall as I had thought him to be from his pictures. I already knew his sister-in-law, since she was living in Belgaum. She had come there as a bride, and had asked me to give her some cooking lessons.

Our tea was buffet style, and we all milled around, filled our plates, balanced our teacups, and then sat at small tables. The General got a cup of tea for himself and came over and sat down at my table. I was surprised, for there were plenty of important people there that he could have spent his time talking to instead of me.

I said to him, "I read in the papers recently that you have just come back from America. Did you like it?"

"Yes, I had a wonderful time. I had always heard that the American people were very friendly, and I found it to be true."

"Did you like the food?"

"Very much. I especially like southern fried chicken. Do you know how to make southern fried chicken?"

"Yes, I do," I answered. "Did you know I've been giving Laltie, your sister-in-law, cooking lessons?"

"No, but that is very nice of you."

"You aren't eating anything," I exclaimed. "Don't you want something more than a cup of tea?"

"No, if I ate every time I appear at some function, I'd be dead."

"It must be tiresome, always being on view," I said. "Wouldn't you just like to disappear sometimes? It must be difficult for you to have someone making a schedule of your every hour of the day. Must make you feel like a puppet."

"Yes, it is tiring at times," he answered and smiled, "but I meet a lot of charming people."

He didn't stay long after that, as he had to appear at another function in his honor, so he excused himself to me, said good-bye to several other people, and left in his car following the roaring motorcycles.

A year later I'd had a baby, gained weight, and couldn't quite get into my yellow suit. Mother Seamands came to visit me for a few days, and while she was there we received a notice from the club that we were again having a tea for General Shrinagesh. This was to be his farewell visit to Belgaum before his retirement from the armed forces. J. T. wasn't at home, so Mother Seamands and I went to the tea.

This time I was not in the receiving line, for I hadn't been on the active club list for a few months. Mother and I were seated on one of the couches in the club when the General and his party came up, helmets, motorcycles, and all. General Shrinagesh had on a dark Jodhpur coat this time. He went around shaking hands with some of the people, but there were too many for him to reach all. They seated him on a couch in the big room, directly across from Mother and me. He spoke a few words to the two men who were seated beside him, glanced across the room and saw us, and promptly got up, came over and said in our American way, "Hello, do you remember me?"

"Hello," I answered. "I certainly do, but I am surprised that you remembered me." I introduced him to Mother Seamands and added, "It's very nice to see you again."

"This is my farewell visit to the military post in Belgaum. I retire after this."

"And I still haven't cooked any American fried chicken for you. Why don't you come to dinner tomorrow evening at my home?"

"I'm sorry, I won't be able to. I'd like very much to come, though."

"Well, I'll keep the invitation open. Next time you visit Belgaum, just come around. I'll have chicken."

The next day I had a note from the secretary of the Officers' Mess, inviting me and the lady who was with me at the tea to dinner that very night. It was then 4:30 in the afternoon, and the dinner was to be at 8:30. That morning, my friend Jo Evans, the doctor's wife from Miraj, had come to visit me. Mother Seamands was coming down with a cold, and she at once said she couldn't go to the dinner. So I persuaded Jo to go with me. I didn't want to go to a big formal dinner alone. J. T. was preaching in some villages. Of course, it is unusual to ask anyone at the last minute to such a formal dinner, and I wondered why they did.

Jo said she would go if we could find a sari and blouse for her to wear. We began madly throwing saris and petticoats and blouses out of a drawer for Jo to try on. Finally she found a white blouse which would fit, and she wore a matching Kashmiri embroidered sari. I wore a black silk blouse with gold threads (the only one I had which would fit my increased proportions) and a green georgette sari with black and gold border.

About a quarter to nine we were ready—baby fed and tucked into bed, Sandy read to and tucked in. Jo and I got into our jeep (dusty, for we had had no time to get it washed) and drove over to the Officers' Mess Hall. It was beautifully decorated, with lights strung out all over the grounds, and the military band in red uniforms playing in the garden. I hated to park the dusty old jeep in front with all the nice cars, and since I didn't see many cars at the side, we parked there.

When Jo and I walked into the huge hall, the place was full of military personnel in spotless white uniforms, with their wives all in gorgeous saris. As we walked in the door, just for an instant there was dead silence. Everybody stopped talking and stared at us, and the quiet was so loud that if I'd dropped my handkerchief, I'd have heard it hit "ping" on the floor. Then the host for the evening, Colonel Faize, showed us to seats, and people started talking again. I whispered to Jo that the silence was a tribute to our stunning beauty.

A lovely Sikh lady whom I knew was sitting next to me, and she too had recently had a new baby, so naturally we talked about our babies. Colonel Faize chatted with us for a while and said, "We are still waiting for the guest of honor."

"Who is the guest of honor this evening?" I asked.

He started to answer, but the roar of two motorcycles gave me the answer. It was the farewell party for General Shrinagesh. It dawned on me then that the engulfing silence when we arrived was simply because everyone was surprised to see us there. We were the only civilians in the whole group. I could see each officer asking himself, "Who invited *them?*"—meaning *us!*

General Shrinagesh came in followed by four handsome young airmen, resplendent in their uniforms, and some other members of his party. He made the rounds of the receiving line, said good-evening to everybody, then came and sat down beside Jo and me on the couch.

"I am very surprised to see you here tonight," I exclaimed.

"Why?"

"Well, because yesterday when I invited you for a chicken dinner, I thought you told me you would be gone by tonight."

"No, I didn't. I told you that I was already engaged for dinner tonight, and that was why I couldn't come to your house. So I had them ask you to come here."

"I noticed that we were the only civilians here!"

"I hope you don't mind, and that you will have a good time."

Jo and I were really elevated in society that night. We talked of lots of things. General Shrinagesh is well educated and stimulating to talk to. I remarked some time later, "Those four young men in uniform who came in with you are very handsome. Who are they?"

"Those? Oh, those are my airmen. Do you think they are good-looking? Which one would you like to meet?"

"Any of them—I mean all of them." I was rather taken aback, but being me, I bubbled, "Well, let me meet the cutest one first. Are they married?"

"Why, I don't know whether they are or not!" Calling two of the airmen over, he introduced them and asked, "Are you married?"

"Yes, we are, but the other two aren't," one of them answered.

"My life is in their hands," the General said. "They fly me everywhere in my private plane."

He called the other two over and asked again, "Are you married?"

One grinned and said, "No, sir, we're not married."

"Well, why aren't you married?" the General probed.

He grinned. "Because I'm too young, sir," he answered.

"My goodness," I exclaimed. "You go up in that plane and take the Colonel everywhere he has to go, but you're too young to get married?"

General Shrinagesh laughed; I didn't know exactly why.

Before dinner, General Shrinagesh pointed out a large photograph on the wall. It was taken on India's Independence Day, when the General was in Japan, and this photo showed him and General Douglas MacArthur standing at attention during the march-past of Indian troops. It was quite impressive to be standing in the middle of such distinction.

We all ate standing up, milling around, and Jo and I talked to the four airmen. They were exceptional young men with polished manners and ready wit. I was thoroughly enjoying the evening in spite of being thirty-nine. We were eating a luscious dessert— fruit with whipped buffalo cream—when General Shrinagesh came up to Jo and me.

"You have no dessert," I said. "Don't you care for any?"

"No, thank you," he answered, "I really eat very little."

"I have something in the ice box at home I bet you would like. It's American chocolate ice cream, and you probably haven't had any since you were in America."

"You have?" he exclaimed. "Good! I'll come over after this party."

Well, you could have knocked me over with a puff. I thought he was joking, and my mouth fell open and I quavered, "Y-you w-will?"

"Of course I will. Do you have a piano?" he asked.

"Yes."

"Good, I'll play you a tune."

The Commander in Chief of all the Armed Forces of India coming to *our* house! My first minute alone with Jo I said, "He said he was coming over after this party!"

"He did?" Jo asked. "How nice." It takes more than a Commander in Chief to ruffle Jo.

Before the party broke up, we all went out in the garden to listen to the band play "Marching Through Georgia," a tune that never fails to amuse me when I hear it played in India. After that we sang "Auld Lang Syne" inside, and then the officers sang "For He's a Jolly Good Fellow" and actually threw General Shrinagesh up in the air and caught him so many times I'm sure he was glad he hadn't eaten much. He was a very good sport about it all, and kept smiling.

The second officer in command that night was a Sikh, a major whose name was Singh. He had had charge of the General's entire program while he was in Belgaum. Major Singh looked extremely handsome in his coat and turban, with his black beard caught and tied in a small net, the way the Sikh officers wear them. Sikhs are stunning people.

We were still standing in a circle after the officers finished singing. Everyone was waiting for the General to leave, for it was not correct protocol for anyone else to leave first. Suddenly, again one of those noisy silences fell, and in this silence, General Shrinagesh walked over to Jo and me and said, "You go first, and I will follow you."

Major Singh was right behind the General, and he leaned over in surprise with his black eyes wide above his black beard and asked, "Did he say he was going to follow *you*?"

"Yes," I answered.

The Major looked as if the floor had suddenly hit him in the stomach and he breathed in shock, "O o o h h." The Major hadn't made that part of the General's program.

Jo and I went out the side door in all our glory, escorted by Major Singh on one side, and Colonel Faize on the other. I backed the jeep, dust and all, to the front where the General's elegant car was waiting. Just as I was about to pull away to lead his car, out in front of all of us roared our two old friends, the motorcycle policemen, complete with helmets without handles.

All this time, Mother Seamands was at home in bed with a cold, and her bedroom was just off the long living room. It was then 11:30 P.M. When our escorts wailed out, I thought they knew where they were going, so I followed them. I started giggling and said to Jo, "If those two policemen go roaring on their motorcycles up into our driveway this time of night, Mother Seamands will come tearing out of bed in her nightgown yelling, 'Whazza matter, whazza matter?' Can't you just see her in her nightgown and with a runny nose, running smack into the Commander in Chief of all the Indian Armed Forces?"

Jo and I laughed so hard at that mental picture that I could hardly see to drive. By this time we were feeling good and silly. We were still rolling slowly through town in the middle of the night—a moonlit night—behind two howling motorcycles.

As we came to an intersection which was like a wheel, with roads going in six directions, the military police turned off into a road which I knew to be a blind alley, so I realized they didn't know where they were going. I turned into the right road, stepped on the accelerator and said, "I'm not going to let them catch me. Maybe we can get home before they wake up Mother Seamands."

I was driving as fast as I dared, and the police lights got closer and closer trying to catch us (to escort us), and just at our gate, when I slowed up a little to turn in, they didn't know I was going to turn, and they roared on past us at such a speed that they were down at the corner before they could turn around.

I slammed on the brakes and told Jo to go and warn Mother what was going on. I saw that Mother's light was on, which meant she was still reading. I waited at the front door for the General who was laughing at the way I had evaded his escort. Jo dashed into Mother's room and said, as the sirens wailed up the drive, "Now don't get alarmed. It is just General Shrinagesh and his party. They are coming in for a while."

Ma Seamands shrieked, "Oh, my goodness!" and reached up and snapped off the light before the General and the good-looking airmen could see her through the crack in the curtain.

The General played a tune on the piano, while I served the chocolate ice cream to him and his friends. Luckily, I had made a lot that day. Then he wanted to see our new baby, so I warned him to be quiet, thinking all the time how funny it was for me, an ordinary dumb American to be telling an Indian general to "be quiet." Then I took him back to the bedroom and showed him both our small redheads, Sandy and baby Linda.

We all talked for a while in the living room then, and I asked the General about his retirement. He told me that he was taking up a post as the head of a college very soon.

"Won't it be strange, Colonel," I asked, "to be just a college president, and not a V.I.P. any more?"

"Yes, it probably will be for a while," he smiled.

"Well, at least you will be able to call your time your own. Any time you come back to Belgaum, let me know and I'll give you that southern fried chicken dinner."

He admired our house and praised the ice cream. Some time after twelve, he said they must go, as he had to be off early the next morning in his plane back to Delhi. He graciously shook hands with us, said "Good night" and left. I said, "Good night, Colonel." I was excited.

After they had gone, Mother Seamands swirled like a tornado out the bedroom door in her nightgown and sniffles and demanded,

"Don't you know any better than *that?* General Shrinagesh is the Commander in Chief of all the Armed Forces in the *whole of India* and you called him *Colonel?* What must he think of you!"

I sank down on the couch and kicked off my shoes. I was uncomfortable, and not because of the shoes, but I hated to admit being so dumb. It must have been the excitement. "Well," I defended myself, "he must like me all right, otherwise he'd have never had us invited to that dinner tonight, nor would he have come over here." I couldn't help but giggle, "I bet it's been a long time since anybody called him 'Colonel.' It ought to keep him from getting high-hat."

"That's the worst I ever heard," Ma Seamands snorted and blew her nose. "You called him 'Colonel.' And you did it more than once! I bet he thinks you're crazy. You'd embarrass the whole American government if the word got spread around."

I wasn't sure whether her tears were because of her cold or because of her stupid daughter-in-law.

"Well," I said cheerfully, "if he knew me better, he'd probably have expected it. You know that I wanted to impress Grandma Shields twenty years ago and prove that her grandson was engaged to an unusual girl, so I fell through the bottom of her fancy chair. I wanted to impress a congregation in Los Angeles and show them what a fine missionary they were supporting, so I appeared in their pulpit for a missionary address and discovered I'd forgotten to take the bobby-pins out of my curly bangs. So now, I want to impress an Indian general with what a friendly American I am and so I call him 'Colonel.' I suppose our government would like to forget I'm an American, if they ever hear about this!"

Probably part of a missionary's education in the future should be a briefing on military jargon.

I can just see myself one fine day, more than a little excited, holding out a plate of fried chicken to General Shrinagesh and saying, "Have a gizzard, Sergeant?"

11

Ten Thousand Black Umbrellas

I stood high on a bridge and watched a sea begin. The ripple started in the center of a dry, white, sandy river bed. As white waves moved out on all sides, they were capped in black. They rolled, whispering, farther and farther from the center; rippling through the sand until it was covered; snaking through rows of small, fragrant tea-stall huts and multicolored bookshops; weaving unevenly up the yellow slopes of the river banks until the sides seemed flecked in black and white foam. The sea rumbled nearer and nearer to my bridge and soon I could distinguish one wave from another. It was a sea of people dressed in white, carrying black umbrellas.

I stood on the bridge at Maraman, in Kerala State, South India. Kerala is the home of the largest annual Christian convention in the world, where, for one week each year, one can see a throng of forty to fifty thousand people attending one service.

According to tradition, the "doubting Apostle," Thomas, after the death of Christ, came to India preaching. His grave can be seen today in Madras. Thomas started the Syrian church, of which the Mar Thoma Church is the evangelical wing. The Mar Thoma Church came out of a reform movement about 150 years ago.

Each year in February, when the water in the river bed is dried,

Pandal at the Maraman Convention, Maraman, South India.

and the sand clean and white, an army of workers from the Mar Thoma Church descends. The men carry large posts which have been stored for the past year, and these they drive in straight rows down into the sand. Then more men and women arrive and begin making a roof. They divide into 250 sections, each group responsible for roofing one section with green, wide-spreading palm branches and leaves. These groups are really different local congregations, for in that 20-mile area around the town of Maraman, there are about 100,000 Christians. This is the home of the Mar Thoma Church, and the most densely Christian-populated area in India.

The emerald shelter (*pandal* as it is called in India) which they make is 350 feet long by 250 feet wide. During the meetings, people spread mats and sit on the ground in straight rows, but crowded close together. There are 250 stewards to receive offerings. Collections are made with bags on the ends of long poles. Each collector is responsible for just one section. A total of about 20,000 rupees (or $5,000) each year is donated, which is used for evangelistic work.

At the three services a day, preaching is usually done in English, but translated into Malayalam. Many in the congregation can understand both languages, so they get the sermon twice. Dr. E. Stanley Jones, one of their favorite evangelists, gave loudspeaking equipment some years ago. Prior to that time, in order that all in the huge tabernacle might hear, the "relay-system" of preaching was used. The preacher spoke a few sentences and waited while the first "relayer," standing about a third of the way back, repeated the sentences to the people farther on. The next "relayer," two-thirds of the way back, took up the message and relayed it on. In this manner it reached all corners of the *pandal* and was then repeated to those on the outside. Now with the loudspeakers, sermons are shorter.

Blazing tropical sun beats down on the green-crowned shelter, and in such heat one would expect to hear fretful children, whimpering at being crowded among so many thousands. Chattering of older children, also might be likely at any other meeting, but not at Maraman. Within this tabernacle all is quiet reverence. Children are taught from an early age that no noise is tolerated here. People come and sit either praying or reading Bibles until service begins, then listen with intensity. There is a smaller overflow shelter, about 75 yards away from the main *pandal* where mothers with babies and very small children must go. A loudspeaker brings the message to them.

Early morning Bible study at seven o'clock has at least two to three thousand people in attendance. Men, women, and young people each have their own groups. Morning and afternoon services are held for the people. Forty to fifty thousand people jam in and around the *pandal*. Evening meetings are for men only, and as many as ten thousand men attend.

Each morning about eight o'clock during the Maraman convention families begin arriving. Very few come by car because of the narrow, dusty roads, pocked with holes, and jammed with thousands of people walking. Some young men come on bicycles as far as possible from their villages but have to leave the cycles at least a half-mile away from the convention site. The only way to move with forty thousand people is to walk with them.

A few camp along the riverbank. Some have small handmade houseboats which they row down the river until the boat is grounded on the powdery sand near Maraman. There they live for the week, and walk the rest of the way to services each day.

Everyone dresses in white. Women wear spotless white saris and blouses. Men wear long, thin white cotton skirts wrapped around their legs, with lengthy white shirts hanging on the outside. Black umbrellas shield them from the glaring sun, and sometimes a whole family will walk under one large umbrella.

When morning and afternoon sessions are concluded, the congregation flows out all sides of the *pandal* and up the river banks. When I stood on the vantage point of the Maraman bridge, it looked as if a black and white sea started with a ripple in a green center.

People bring their lunch to the morning service, and afterwards eat while sitting on the river bank under palm trees. They buy their drink and dessert from the tea shops and sweets stalls which spring up some distance away from the tabernacle. There are strict rules as to how close to the *pandal* any kind of shop can be set up.

I know that Billy Graham draws bigger crowds, but this convention is this large every year. It started in 1896. All the ministers of the Mar Thoma Church, their bishops, including the head bishop, the Metropolitan, attend services the whole week. Colorful red robes with black sashes distinguish the bishops. They also wear black skullcaps, embroidered in white and gold. A small piece of black cloth sewn on the back of the cap just brushes their shoulders.

The Metropolitan's robe is purple, with a black sash. The bishops and Metropolitan all wear flowing beards. They do not marry. Members of the Mar Thoma Church show great love and respect to these leaders.

J. T. has been invited several times to be one of the two main speakers at Maraman. He has worked at different times there with Dr. E. Stanley Jones, Dr. Bob Pierce, Dr. Paul S. Rees, and the late Dr. Donald Barnhouse. Dr. E. Stanley Jones goes back every other year.

Usually, walking would be difficult in a gathering of this kind in India, because of the beggars. They are everywhere, many so maimed they cannot move. They gather by hundreds at any religious occasion, knowing that people, mellowed by a religious address, will be generous with their money. At Maraman, beggars are not allowed close to the tabernacle. About a quarter of a mile away, a special place is provided for them. Collections are taken at the meetings throughout the week for beggars, and they are fed.

As one walks through the beggar area, the choking stench of disease and unwashed bodies assails the nostrils, and every kind of gruesome sight meets the eyes. Children, deliberately maimed at birth, are made to beg; all kinds of people misshapen by birth defects, and some dozens of lepers in various stages of the disease (many with their eyes, ears, noses, toes, fingers or hands missing) are there. Others are victims of the dread disease elephantiasis. Each one of them has some part of his body swollen, perhaps to ten times the normal size.

Some of the Mar Thoma ministers visit these shelters and preach to the beggar population during the week. No doubt it is the only time in their lives they hear a Christian message.

As to the results of this convention, who can measure? Its influence touches the whole Mar Thoma Church and more.

Each year on Friday morning, part of the offering is the offering of lives. A sermon of dedication is preached, and parents who wish to dedicate any of their children to the ministry bring them forward. Then the bishops lay hands on the children and bless them, dedicating them to God's service.

One such boy was Kunjukutty Athialy. Some thirty-five years ago, the great Indian Christian, Sadhu Sundar Singh, was preaching at Maraman. Sundar Singh had just completed a trip into Nepal and was deeply concerned over the great spiritual need in that "closed land." He made such an impassioned plea for missionaries that a young Indian mother brought her baby boy forward and dedicated him as a future missionary to Nepal.

As soon as the lad was able to speak a few words, the mother taught him this prayer, which he repeated every night during his boyhood: "Lord Jesus, when I become a big boy, please send me as a missionary to Nepal."

Of course Athialy didn't realize all that was involved in this simple prayer, but somehow there came into his heart such a love for the country of Nepal that he longed even to touch the soil of the country with his hands. Often he looked at the map of Nepal and whispered to himself, "That's where I'm going some day."

After finishing high school, Athialy entered the Union Biblical Seminary in Yeotmal, Central India. He interested one of his classmates in Nepal also. My husband and I were present at Athialy's graduation exercises. At this time, J. T., along with some other missionaries, laid hands on these two young men and consecrated them for mission work in Nepal.

We missionaries present were so impressed with the two young men and their testimonies that we took up an offering for them to help them on their journey. They thanked us warmly for the offering, but said they could not take it. They must be supported in Nepal by their own church, the Mar Thoma, for no one in Nepal must think that they were being supported by foreign funds. Their effectiveness might be jeopardized. So we sent the offering to the Mar Thoma Church for them.

Athialy is an effective minister in Nepal today. Likewise, many others, dedicated as children in Maraman, are witnessing for Christ today throughout India and other parts of the world.

So the sea of white and black flows out of the emerald *pandal* at Maraman, and its waves ripple round the world.

12

Waves of Influence
~~
At Home in the Zoo

It is a cliche to say "the world is getting smaller every day and what is done anywhere effects everybody else." Yet it is so true: it was constantly being brought to my attention.

Joseph, my cook, went to the bazaar every day to buy vegetables and meat, and always came home and told me the gossip and talk in the bazaar. That's how I kept up with the world. One day he came home and said, "Mem-Sahib, don't go down to the bazaar today; and not for quite a while. People there are mad at the Americans."

I was surprised. "What are they mad about?"

"Well, you know, not very long ago, America set off some atomic bombs to test them. But the wind blew them back over India, and has brought Asian flu. Half the people in Belgaum are sick, and hospitals are overcrowded. People are dying too, some in the hospital yards because there aren't enough beds, and we don't have enough doctors to take care of them."

Of course, I had known that the Asian flu was spreading over India—it was in the papers every day. Our doctor friends were working day and night. I said, "Joseph, do they really blame the Americans for the Asian flu?"

"Yes," he answered. "People in bazaar say if America didn't

shoot off all those atomic bombs we wouldn't have Asian flu. So
don't go to bazaar today, they are mad at American people and
they might hurt you." Joseph didn't look any too happy to be
working for Americans just then.

I stayed away from the bazaar and didn't feel too comfortable
as long as the flu raged in town. Then a few months later, the
farmers planted their crops of rice, and the monsoons began. It
rained and rained, much harder than usual; floods were all over
India and many farmers in our area lost all their crops. It meant
famine for the end of the year.

One day Joseph came back from the bazaar smiling, "It's all right
for you to go to bazaar now, Mem-Sahib. People not mad at the
Americans any more. Now they are mad at the Russians."

"Well, that's a relief. But what have the Russians done?"

"You know about two weeks ago the Russians shot up a rocket
and it had a dog in it? Well, bazaar people are saying they shot
off the rocket *so far,* that the dog went *so high* that it poked a
hole up there and caused all this rain and floods. So they are mad
at the Russians and you can go to bazaar when you want to. Everybody knows you're American."

So sometimes it was difficult for us missionaries to "live down"
the effects of things which happen in America, because most people
think America is all Christian. We read in the newspapers of the
increase of social drinking and alcoholism in America, yet in India,
Prime Minister Nehru had declared that he did not believe in
"cocktail diplomacy" and issued an order that Indian embassies
abroad should not serve liquor at their parties and functions.

Among the Christians in India, Dr. E. Stanley Jones made a
slogan popular. He held up three fingers and said that they stood
for "Jesus Is Lord." But in American advertising the Christians
saw people holding up three fingers to advertise a fine beer!

Another influence we had to live down was that of Hollywood
films. The only impression that many people in India have of the

United States is what they get in movies, and that is a distorted picture of an America full of sex, divorce, and crime. That isn't very complimentary to the Christian standard on marriage, chastity, and the value of human life. The Indian board of film censors is very strict, and they cut out hundreds of feet of American film before allowing certain pictures to be shown. Sometimes though, Hollywood has produced something magnificent like *The Ten Commandments,* or *Sound of Music.* The film *A Man Called Peter* had a tremendous influence for good in India.

Indians are quick to remind us too of the history of wars which the so-called "Christian nations" have started. The Burmese say that their religion, Buddhism, is much better, because it never started a war.

So that's how it is. Missionaries and Americans in a foreign country are often embarrassed and hindered by the sins of their own people. We simply have to admit that many practices in America are not at all Christian.

Our kids were not concerned with those grave problems. They were most concerned about our zoo. In the beginning, we only had a couple of love birds, an Irish setter, two cocker spaniels and a horse of an unknown breed. That was it until one day the headman of a village, a good friend of J. T.'s, sent a messenger to tell us he had captured two small deer in the jungle and wanted to give them to the children. J. T. and I stood there discussing whether to accept them, and I said to the village man, "But we don't have any place to keep them."

We were standing in our living room, and he pointed over to one corner where one of my Persian rugs was lying and said, "That is a very good place to keep them at night, and you can tie them outside in the daytime."

I got the giggles over that, but he didn't see anything funny in bringing animals into your house at night. Everybody does that in villages.

Of course, as soon as the children heard it, they began to beg for the deer, so we told them the deer would be their coming-home present. Their school year had just ended in October, so they were home from their boarding school for a long Christmas vacation. The next day we drove to the village in our jeep station-wagon and returned with the two deer in the back. Sheila sat on the floor with them, holding the male deer's head on her jeans-covered lap. She didn't want them to be frightened.

We really didn't have enough room for a zoo. We had to keep the jeep outside, and tie the two deer in one corner of the garage and the horse in the other. I said one day, "Next, we'll have to move out of the bungalow and add an elephant. Come to think of it, I've always wanted a baby elephant. Of course, we need a parrot too."

That village headman must have been psychic! The next day somebody called me to the front door, and there stood the same man who had given us the deer. He hadn't brought a baby elephant, though I really wouldn't have been surprised, but a parrot.

We just happened to have a cage left over from the love birds, who had moved into a more spacious dwelling, so we put the parrot, whom we called Popeye, into it. Sylvia gave Popeye half a banana, and he ate it right out of her hand without taking a finger too. Meanwhile, Sheila and Sandy were feeding slices of bread to the deer whom they called Bambie and Flower. Our birds' names were Goldie and Chirpie; the dogs were called Blackie, Lucky, and Rosie; the horse's name was Rusty. Sheila also had a guinea hen who slept on the roof every night in outright defiance of the civet cats and snakes. But the guinea hen made so much noise that I once said to Sheila, "If that hen doesn't simmer down, she's going to find herself simmering in a stew some day!"

Sheila was horrified to think I would stew her pet in a pot.

I was stunned after realizing all the mouths I had to feed on a missionary's salary.

Of course, we had some "naturals" which we didn't feed, but which joined us anyhow. They were the big black-faced white-whiskered monkeys which jumped across our roof continually, breaking tiles so that every monsoon season we had to buy more buckets to catch the leaks.

Then there were the ever-present cobras sliding around the grounds. There were the small, striped kraits—tiny, deadly snakes, which adored the coolness of our bathroom's stone floors; also scorpions, though we didn't have too many of those. There were the jungle cats which occupied our attic and fought with the rats which occupied the whole house. Out in the yard we had a small family of mongoose who killed the snakes. We loved them! Sometimes we looked up into our eight skylight windows high above our living room, and in every window we could see several monkey faces, just peering down at us, as if they were free and we were in the cage. An eerie feeling! Our old house always rocked when the children came home from boarding school, but with our zoo it hummed, cawed, whinnied, barked, whistled, and shrieked. My mother wrote a poem about it for the kids:

Home on the Mission Compound

(To the tune of "Home On The Range")

Oh, give me a home where the elephants roam,
And the deer and the cobras all play,
Where the chatter of monkeys quite often is heard
And the parakeet sings all the day.

Chorus:
    Home—on the mission compound,
    Where there's always some new thing each day.
    Where seldom is heard an American word,
    And the buffalos roam the highway.

Oh, give me a spot where it always is hot,
Where the dogs and the pony hold sway,
Where the parrot won't speak, but pouts for a week,
Because he has nothing to say.

Oh, give me some food to feed all this brood;
Some corn and some oats and some hay,
A bone for poor Blackie and Lucky and Rose,
But the cobras can just crawl away!

Oh, give me a site, where the rain comes at night,
And leaks through the roof on my bed,
Where my poor husband's hats are eaten by rats,
And the jungle cat stalks overhead!

                                    Pearl Childers

13

Diary of a Jungle Ride
~~
Some Table Instructions

I'm sitting in a jungle "traveler's cottage"; something like a one-house motel which travelers can rent for about twenty-five rupees per night. There are four rooms here and eight beds with very thin mattresses. Of course, we bring our own bedding rolls, and also our own food. There is a servant who stays on the place and who will heat water for tea or coffee for us, but he does not cook any food. So our supper last night was cold except for a cup of hot tea.

The children and J. T. are rolling up the bedding rolls and re-packing our food basket, and soon we will be on our way up the mountains to Kodaikanal. It is time to take the children back to boarding school, so we all came along because we wanted to take an elephant ride in the jungle. The children have wanted to do this for a long time.

These elephants here at this camp are work elephants. They drag teakwood logs out of the jungle to the camp and lift them onto trucks. But if one gets up very early, he can have a ride on an elephant through the jungle before they put the elephant to work for that day.

Last night after supper we went down to the jungle stream to watch the elephants and their babies take baths. The babies were so entertaining, splashing in the stream, blowing water, and making noises at each other. Elephants have to have baths every day. They soak for quite a while—an hour or more—in a stream because of certain kinds of ticks which work their way into the elephant's skin if they don't bathe each day. There were about twelve or fifteen elephants in the river last night, and the keepers were scrubbing their wrinkled skins with long brushes. When a keeper wanted to scrub the head and ears, the elephant picked the keeper up and put him on his head, long brush and all. After watching them last night I decided I wouldn't mind having a baby elephant for a pet in our zoo.

It is much colder at night in this jungle than I ever thought it would be, so we had to sleep in part of our clothes, even our sox. This morning when we had to roll out before daylight at 5:15, I grumbled because I was cold, because I didn't have any hot food for breakfast, and because we were paying twenty-five rupees to get hauled out of bed at such an unearthly hour. The servant brought us some hot water for tea, so we ate our third meal of cold beans and cold sliced beef (from cows so tough the beef had to be roasted all day) and hard bread, drank our tea, and went down the hill.

Our elephant, Sabu, was waiting for us. He was decorated with some paint around his eyes and trunk, and on his back was a sling arrangement with seats on both sides. Six could sit there at once, three on each side. We were even in luxury because they had put foam rubber cushions on the seats. To get up onto the seats we had to climb up a ladder. I never realized before how big an elephant is, even when lying on the ground.

When we were settled in the seats, the elephant rose up off the ground in all his bulky majesty. We were first tossed backward and then forward and had to hold hard onto the railing of the sling seats. When he had finished unfolding his legs and was standing, we were about twelve feet in the air, and we could see far, far up over the top of the tall jungle grass in the early dawn.

The driver sat on the elephant's head, between its ears, and guided the animal by constantly scratching its ears with his bare toes. If he wanted it to go right, he scratched the left ear, and vice versa.

We rode right through the jungle for three hours and ten minutes, not on jungle trails but in unmarked areas, making our own trails. Two trackers were walking here and there ahead of us, swinging their machetes, looking for wild animal tracks. The purpose of our ride was to see, at our safe height, some wild animals at the watering holes in the early morning.

The trackers looked very small down among the tall grass, some of which grew from eight to twelve feet high. When we came to a tree in our path and which was too big for the machetes to cut down, our elephant, Sabu, just picked it up in his trunk, lifted it out of the ground, roots and all, and tossed it aside like a match. Sometimes branches of trees snapped back into our faces, so we always had to be alert.

Our trackers found two herds of wild bison, so we stopped and watched them at the watering hole. We saw a lone mother elephant staked out with her new baby. The baby came near us and the children wanted to pet it, but the mother didn't look as if she cared to share her baby. We saw many different kinds of deer, some small and spotted, and some big with branches of horns. I really wanted to see a tiger or leopard, but we didn't. I suppose they slink close to the ground and could have been very near, but we couldn't have spotted them through the thick grass.

We crossed several whispering streams winding through the jungle, and when Sabu started across, we were first tossed forward nearly over his head as he started down the steep bank; then when he went up the bank on the opposite side, we had to hold onto each other and to the railing to keep from sliding back over his tail.

By the time we'd been riding three hours, the sun was high and beating down on us; we were stiff and glad to come down to earth again. Now it is nearly time to go; the bedding rolls are packed into the jeep trailer, and J. T. is putting on the tarpaulin and ropes. The children have had such fun this vacation that they hate to go back into boarding school. I can hardly bear to have them go. It will be four months before I see them again. Mothers should be with their children more than this!

While coming through Bangalore two days ago, we stopped in a restaurant, and on each table was a little booklet of instructions to the patrons. We were so tickled at the instructions that we had a hard time eating. I brought a booklet along with me to give to any of my friends who don't know how to behave in a restaurant.

Here in India, many people are coming in from villages to find work in cities, but they bring their village habits with them and do not know how to behave in a city, so this set of instructions is printed to make life easier for other patrons. The English is not perfect, but it is graphic. The funny thing is that some of the very people who need these instructions the most cannot read a word.

OUR APPEAL

Health is Wealth by itself.

Cleanliness is the foundation for good health.

Observation of certain important principles become inevitable to keep a place clean to where hundreds of people rush. Such a list of rules is not meant to wound anybody's feelings, it is only a means to serve all, in the best possible manner.

1. Please do not spit in the premises or in any other way make place insanitary. Such insanitary acts spread diseases. Kindly do not be a cause for and a prey to diseases.

2. It is harmful to lean back on or to touch the walls of the building. Insecticide to destroy bugs, ants and cockroaches, etc. is mixed with the whitewash on the wall.

3. Remember, you will be a source of trouble to your fellow customers and hinderance to the proper catering if you disturb the arrangement of chairs. So please do not do this.

4. Please do not rest your legs on the chair since this will soil

the neat dress of another customer who comes after.

5. Let your voice be low so that people unconcerned with your conversation may not be disturbed.

6. Please order the item that is ready just at the moment if you are in a hurry.

7. Please do not throw the curry leaves or other ingredients of the foodstuff either on the floor or on the table; leave them in the plate.

8. We request our patrons to keep the cups and spoons in the saucers and not on the tables. Farther they are requested to avoid the use of saucer for drinking coffee or tea.

And therefore, use the saucer right beneath the cup so that drops of coffee may not fall on your cloths.

Before you drink stir in the cup with spoon to dissolve the sugar.

After you drink, keep the spoon and the cup in the saucer.

9. Respect the feelings of your neighbors before you smoke. Put the ash and butt end of cigarette in the ash tray.

10. Please do not spit or gargle or blow your nose in the wash basin—Spit and other semi-fluid matters hinder the dirty water being drained off from the basin to the gutter smoothly. They also make the customers nearby shrug their shoulders in dislike.

11. Do not waste water, precious and costly as it is in this water-scarce Bangalore. Close the tap immediately after use.

12. Please make payment on the table and obtain the balance before you leave your seat.

We earnestly request to cooperate with us in keeping the premises clean, beautiful and attractive by scrupulously observing the rules mentioned above. We shall be extremely happy to receive helpful suggestions from our patrons. Thank you,

PROPRIETOR

14

Road Sights

Traveling in India is a tiring, hot, and dusty experience, but if we try, we can forget the heat and dust by enjoying what we pass. We are so used to seeing everything else in the roads in India (except a lot of cars) that we sometimes don't *see* them any more. Driving is so automatic that we just go on by, with one great wish —that the slow moving things would *not* keep in the center of the road. It is a vain wish, however, for the center of the road is the best place. It is the best place for walking in bare feet, best for cattle hooves, and best for the monkeys to play.

We drove from Kodaikanal to Bangalore, and for 260 miles of the trip I marked down an account of all the different things we had to dodge in the road. This account does not include cattle grazing *alongside* the road which amounted to many hundreds. This only includes things and people which were *in the road*, which meant slowing down for, and sometimes completely stopping for. Marking this account kept me busy the whole day; I had no opportunity to take a nap or be a back-seat driver. I was making little lines in groups of fives alongside my traffic list.

We steered around 475 bullock carts, all going at the terrific speed of 3 miles per hour. In about half the carts the drivers were asleep; the bullocks were plodding along by themselves. Drivers simply get their caravan started down the road, and the bullocks keep moving, always in the center and very slow to move to one side or the other; then, of course, we never know which side they will choose. We heard a story of a village man who was going to drive all night in his cart to get to a market, so he started his bullocks in the right direction and promptly went to sleep. Some friends played a trick on him, turned the bullocks around in the middle of the road, and so they went all night in the opposite direction!

The next interesting thing of note was that we passed 342 *bunches* of cattle. Some of these were big herds, some just two or three at a time. We couldn't possibly count the cattle singly. When there was a herd in the middle of the road, some would run to the right side of the road and some to the left, but there was always one which changed its mind at the last minute and dashed across the road just as we started up again.

We passed 168 cars in the 260 miles; these were mostly buses and trucks; very few were individual cars. The roads in this area are only good in the middle. The sides slope, so when passing another car, we must always get two of our wheels off the road. If we are passing a truck which is heavily loaded, the driver will never move over to the side, for it would tip his load too much. We must stop clear off the road and wait for him to go by. Bus drivers are more polite, and when they can hear a horn over the roar of their own engines, they will pull over and wave us on.

Though the roads in India are nothing like our highways, many of them have been paved recently and are in fairly good shape now. One nice thing is that, in many sections, avenues of trees have been planted along either side. This shade is a welcome relief from the long stretches of burning heat.

After driving for about three hours, we came to barren countryside, just like a desert. It never fails. "Daddy, I have to go to the bathroom."

No rest rooms at all, not for hundreds of miles in India, so J. T. answered, "You'll just have to wait until I find a tree or bush somewhere."

In an angelic singsong voice, "You'd better stop, Daddy, you'll be sorry!"

Not a car in sight. We stopped. Then over the hill came a whole convoy. No help for that. Daddy wasn't sorry he stopped.

We counted up to 875 bicycles, then I quit. This does not include any in any towns, just 875 bicycles on country roads! All coming at high speed, many weaving all over the road, and often with two passengers. Sometimes they keep to their own side; sometimes at the last minute the cyclist will weave to the other side, right in the path of the car. There was one cycle weaving in front of us like that, and the rear passenger, a little boy, fell off. The next thing we knew the driver of the cycle landed on his nose in a thorn bush growing alongside the road.

There were 69 monkeys in the road all playing and having a dust party. They looked so human we almost forgot to count them. Lots of mother monkeys were leaping around, playing tag, with their babies clinging to their stomachs.

There were three wheelbarrows trundling down the country road; speed, one mile per hour.

Pigs made a nice fat showing too. There were 19 of them. Some of these 19 were in groups of two or three, but mostly they were alone.

There were 27 donkeys carrying an assortment of things. One was carrying a bunch of chickens on its back. The rest were carrying laundry, men, and firewood.

Crows were everywhere, many sitting in the road. One crow was pecking at a dead rat. Evidently the crow thought its flight timing was perfect, but it didn't reckon with our jeep, so we hit it. Dead crow and dead rat lay together, waiting for the next crow to come along.

Many quails in the road.

One happy little driving hazard was a large hand cart filled with eight-foot lengths of water pipe, being pushed down the middle of the road by two sweating men.

Of horses and horse-carts we didn't keep any count—too numerous.

We came around at least two dozen bridges under repair, each complete with its own dusty, bumpy detour.

In one jungle area there was a big five-foot cobra slithering across the road. We ran over it, but didn't kill it. Looking back, we saw it disappear into the bushes at the side.

Scattered throughout all these 260 miles full of bullock carts, donkeys, buses, trucks, quails, crows, monkeys, and cattle were people walking—hundreds and hundreds of village people walking down the road. They walk on the good part because it is easier on bare feet. Sometimes they don't hear the horn because their turbans are tied low over their ears so tightly. Then when they do hear it, they quickly decide they are on the wrong side of the road, and dart across in front of us at the last moment.

These village people carry their burdens on their heads, and I wrote down some of the different things I saw them carrying. They were balancing vegetables, coconuts, firewood, fruit, rope, oil, grain. One lady was just carrying an old tin can upside down. There were water pots, mats, cloth, grass, bamboo poles, brooms, cow dung in baskets, stones and dirt in baskets, umbrellas, brass pieces, oil drums, and milk cans. We saw all the things on that list just in the space of half an hour. Wonder what we'd have seen if we'd noticed all day? In one village there were two women squatting by the side of the road, one picking lice out of the other's hair.

All these things I've mentioned are driving hazards of course, but in comparison to the highway death rate in America, this kind of hazard is not so great as that of speed demons and drunks in

America. We develop a sense of caution in India, because we know all those obstacles will be in the road, and we know we cannot go fast. I remember one furlough in America: The first time I drove after being in India for six and a half years, I was scared to death. Driving in India seemed so much safer with all the slow things in the road.

After making a total of all the animals and cars we had passed during the day, the question we asked each other was, "How in the world did we ever make that trip in only ten hours?"

15

Customs and Christians

Kipling once said, "Oh, East is East and West is West and never the twain shall meet." When we first arrived in India, it seemed to me that what he said was absolutely true. The Indian people did everything in the opposite way to which we would do it.

For instance, we drive on the right side of the road, but in India they drive on the left. The American farmer milks his cow from the right side (of the cow, that is) but the Indian farmer milks from the left. In America it is "ladies first," but in India it is "men first." When a villager walks along the road, he usually walks a few paces ahead of his wife, and she comes behind with the luggage. (J. T. was raised in India, and though I don't have to carry the luggage, he still forgets to walk *with* me; he always walks ahead). At meal time the male members of the family are fed first, and then the ladies eat.

I've often thought that if St. Paul had been an American and had been married, he'd have had to rescind some of his statements on women. Otherwise he'd have been faced with outright anarchy in his home when his wife proofread his manuscripts. But in India he'd have fitted very well.

In America when we go to church, the men take off their hats but keep their shoes on. In India, when a man goes to his temple or mosque, he takes off his shoes and keeps his hat on.

Our poetry rhymes at the end of the line, but much of the Indian poetry rhymes at the beginning of the line.

In America, it is the women who have the variety of hair styles and hats, but in India the women wear no hats, and the majority of them have the same style hairdo. It is the men who wear a great variety of hats and do their hair in different styles. The Orthodox Hindu wears a long tuft of hair at the crown of his head. The Sikhs wear long hair and beards—they never shave nor cut their hair—but keep their hair under a turban, and they tie up their beards in neat little nets.

In America young people fall in love and then get married, but in India, first they get married and when they grow up and live together they are supposed to fall in love. The parents choose the life partners for their children. This happens all the time, but here is an illustration of someone we know very well.

One of the boys in my boarding school was named Shanth. When he was seven or eight years old, he was "married" to a baby who was then only a few months old. She was his own first cousin. Of course they didn't live together then; his father sent him to our boarding school where he grew up. After they both grew up, he and she were married again by Christian rites before they lived together. J. T. baptized their third baby when we were there just a year and a half ago.

After their real marriage, Shanth sent his wife to high school, which she finished. The "marriage" at first was not a marriage at all. Shanth's brother was being married properly by Christian rites. His father wanted to have no more marriage expenses, so he let the little eight-year-old Shanth "listen" to the older brother's ceremony. The baby girl that Shanth was supposed to have married then wasn't even there. But for all those years they were really considered married.

The differences in customs even reaches to the shaking of one's head. In America it means "no," but in India it means "yes."

When I go to sleep at night, I draw the covers up to my chin and keep my feet covered up. But the Indian villager will sleep with his head completely swathed in his blanket, and his bare feet sticking out every time.

In America when you are invited out for a meal, the hostess serves the dessert last, but in India the sweet is first. And eating with the fingers is perfectly all right there. In America belching is considered bad manners and we always ask pardon, but in India, in order to show the hostess you really enjoyed the food, a good hearty belch or two is perfectly in order and is appreciated by the hostess.

Though our customs and habits would seem to separate us, when we are Christians there is an immediate bond of fellowship with the Indian people. We love them and they know it, and they love us. Indians are very friendly; they have a good sense of humor and see a joke quickly. We can never visit their homes and leave without drinking or eating something. Many of their customs and habits are amusing to us, as I am sure ours are to them. When they are converted, many of them have to face persecution such as we never have to face. To many of them it really *means* something to be a Christian.

We in America have a lot to learn from the Indian people, and over the years I learned lessons on humility, faith and prayer. Nearly all the Indian people are extremely religious. It is easy to talk about religion, for everyone is interested in the subject and is glad to tell what he knows about his god. And they practice their religion so openly. A Hindu stops at his temple right on a busy street and bows down to pray, putting flowers or some other offering at the feet of his god. We saw this all the time at a little wayside shrine which was just a block from our home in Belgaum. We've been in Mohammedan shops when it is time to pray (five times a day) and the proprietor would excuse himself and go have his prayers. We've been in trains when a man would put his prayer rug on the floor and go through his prayers, oblivious to all others in the compartment.

They take their religion into everything they do in life. Once we were having some Hindu coolies build a new room onto our house. When the time came to put in the door frame, the men wanted to have some religious ceremony as is their custom. Normally such a ceremony would call for the breaking of a coconut, offering of flowers, and smearing some saffron powder on the door frame, all in the name of their god.

Naturally, it would have been a bit embarrassing to have such a Hindu rite taking place in a Methodist parsonage, so J. T. hesitated to give them permission to do it. But he did appreciate their sincere desire to mix their religion and their work. So he made the suggestion that he read a passage from our Holy Book and offer a prayer of thanksgiving to God in their own language. This satisfied them. They stood holding the door frame ready to be put into the new room while J. T. read the Scripture and prayed. After the prayer, they happily put in the frame.

Every religion has a sacred book. One day J. T. and I were in an Indian shop when I heard an old man mumbling in the corner of the room. I asked the shopkeeper what the old "Tata" (grandfather; a term of respect) was doing. He told me that the old man, who was a very devout Mohammedan, had memorized the entire Koran from beginning to end. That would be just like memorizing the whole Bible. Each day the old man recited a chapter or two until he got through the book. Then he started all over again.

Some outstanding conversions in India have taken place solely through reading the New Testament, or some Gospel portion. Many converts never met a missionary and never heard a sermon, but were led to Christ through the Scriptures.

The Gospel of John one day found its way into the hands of a fifteen-year-old boy. He belonged to a very strict Muslim family, and he was not permitted to read the Christians' Book. But he was curious to know just what it was in the Book that he wasn't supposed to read, so he began to read it secretly in the privacy of his room. The Holy Spirit spoke to him through the words of the gospel, convicted him of his sinfulness, and convinced him that Jesus is truly the Saviour of the world. He was converted. When he told his parents he had become a Christian, they were terribly angry, and disowned him—even drove him away from home. But this young boy kept true to Christ, continued his education in a mission school, and later went on to seminary. He is Bishop John Subhan, now retired, but formerly our bishop in South India. He was the first convert from Mohammedanism to be elected a bishop of the Methodist church in the world.

Indian villagers have a simple faith that sometimes puts our lack of faith to shame. When a villager's animals are sick, he puts his hands on them and prays for them. Sick animals have been brought to J. T. and he has been asked to pray for them. After all, the average farmer in India is so poor that if he owns one buffalo and a few chickens he is lucky. The death of one of these animals or fowls would be a tremendous blow to the family's economy. So if even a chicken is sick, they pray. When anyone loses anything, he asks God to help him locate it.

In India we see giving until it really hurts. Many Christians tithe everything they have, so at harvest time they take two bags out to the field to gather in the crop. The first nine handfuls of grain they put in their own bag. The tenth they put in "God's bag." This they give to the church.

At our thanksgiving offering, we really have some unusual offerings—those which would never fit into a collection plate. One person may bring down a goat and tie it at the altar, where it stands "baaa-ing." Another may bring chickens whose cluckings intersperse the "baas." Some bring pumpkins, bags of rice, jowar, wheat, some ghi (clarified butter), squash, or homemade sweets.

These are later sold and the money put into the church funds. We've even seen village women take off their silver toe-rings and drop them into the collection plate. This is a great sacrifice for any woman, for her jewelry is a sign her husband loves her.

Sometimes Indian Christians give even their very lives. Sometimes their homes are burned to the ground when they are converted and leave the Hindu community. We know a minister in the Bombay Conference whose mother tried to poison him because she felt disgraced when he became a Christian.

To see some of these people stand victoriously against so much opposition makes me ashamed that I am not a better Christian. Yes, Indians often pay a great price for the Christianity we sometimes take so lightly.

16

A Day With My Angels

Heaven isn't heaven without all the angels, and for nine months out of every year, two of our four angels had to be sent 800 miles away to boarding school. It was the only way to insure them an education in the English language, and in American subjects. Each year then, after several lonely months of hard work on the hot plains of South India, J. T., Sandy, baby Linda, and I used to go up the Palni mountains, up 7000 feet to Kodaikanal, take our two children out of boarding for a month and send them to day school. It was our vacation. But after so long without them, we had to get acquainted all over again. Sylvia and Sheila exclaimed over Sandy's growth, and how smart our baby was to whistle so early. Our apartment rocked with the furor of getting reacquainted.

My two larger angels always needed repairs. Sleeves were outgrown, hems were scalloped up with safety pins, bangs below eyelash level, sox were mismated, and shoes full of holes. I was a missionary, yes, but I was a mama first, and being with my children —even with so many repairs to make—meant happiness for me.

Our oldest daughter, Sylvia, has always wanted to be a doctor, and after she had had one year of biology in high school, she knew a great deal about the human body. I had to be very explicit when describing any of my many symptoms to her. On her second day home she had a pain in her midsection, and I placidly remarked, "You probably have worms."

"No," she replied thoughtfully, "I think I have a valve spasm, and I'm not sure that roast appeals to me."

I was putting lunch on the table. After dormitory food for four months, Sylvia and Sheila had requested three four-course meals every day. They were never filled up.

I called the rest of the family to lunch. J. T. is brilliant, of course, and I'm lucky to have him for the father of my children, but he can never remember where he put the jeep keys, and many other things. While we were eating that day, he was expounding to us a lecture on Theistic Evolution at the same time he was eating a roast goat sandwich. Oh yes, we eat roast mutton in India —only it usually turns out to be goat. Anyway, Sandy thought the sandwich looked good and said, "Daddy, make me one."

Between snatches of discourse on deep theological truths (in simple English) he piled on a piece of bread two juicy slices of roast goat, some mustard (to temper the taste), home-made pickles, a slice of tomato, and a lettuce leaf. He was still deep in thought and argument when Sandy's plaintive voice broke in, "Daddy! You made that sandwich for me and now you've eaten it all up!"

A twist of bread crust, a curl of lettuce, and a few drops of pickle juice dripped from his dedicated fingers.

Sheila and Sylvia (valve spasm and all) went back to school and two Indian children came in to play with Sandy. I told them to play in the guest room so they wouldn't wake up baby Linda. In a few minutes Sandy came in and said sternly, "Mommy, you told us to play in the guest room. Well, in the guest room there is a devil, in the living room there is a ghost, and on the veranda there is a naughty girl, and in the tree there is a cobra. Now where shall we play?"

I supposed I could handle the devil easier than the others, so I told her to go back and tell the devil he was in a missionary's house and to get out. She went to the door of the guest room and yelled in the Kanarese language, "Hey, devil! Get out of here. This is a mission house and we're going to play church. You are in the wrong place!"

Evidently the devil understood Kanarese and left for more hospitable surroundings, for in a few minutes the children were playing happily in the guest room.

I like fried chicken for supper. I like it better when it is served with stimulating conversation. Our chicken that night was excellent, or it started out to be. While I was enjoying a tasty morsel of crispy, white meat, doused liberally with high-calorie gravy, Sylvia said, "Mother, I had a super time in biology today. I anaesthetized a frog and cut it open while the heart was still beating. I studied especially its heart and lungs. Did you ever see the inside of a frog?"

My stomach lurched and I laid down the chicken. "No, I didn't! Please change the subject and let me enjoy this chicken, though it seems suddenly to have lost its flavor. Sheila, would you like a leg?"

"Speaking of chicken and frogs and things, Mother," Sheila answered, "do you know how a duck-billed platypus feeds its young?"

I swallowed some gravy again and mentally quieted my queasy stomach. "No, how? Like every other animal, I suppose."

"A platypus is not an animal; it's a mammal." Sheila glowed with knowledge. "It hatches eggs, though, by carrying them around under its tail. To feed the young, it secretes milk in little pouch-like parts, and the young lap it up like dogs. Please pass another chicken leg."

"I am *tired* of frogs' hearts and platypusses' pouches," I said firmly. "Now change the subject to something calm and digestive, and let me enjoy this chicken!"

"Something digestive," mused Sylvia with naughty eyes, "something perhaps like gastric juices, bile, and acids. Mother—" she broke off, "don't eat so much of that gravy. It's too fattening!"

"You stick to your gastric juices and frogs' hearts," I muttered, "and I'll take care of this gravy."

"Mother," Sheila asked between bites, "will you pop some corn tonight?"

I sighed, thinking with longing of how I'd like to read in bed. "I still have a lot of work to do. If I'm not too tired, maybe."

"Please say yes. Just pop a little, please?"

"Well, if I feel like it."

Rolling her eyes heavenward, Sheila sought higher help, intoning, "Oh Lord, let her feel like it!" Then coming back to earth again with a sigh she said sadly, "Today is my last day as president of my class. Miss Liddle says I'm just the type to be president."

"Too bad you can't be President of the United States," her father said.

"Why not, Daddy? Oh yes, because I'm a girl. I hate to give my presidency up. Oh well, I've had a good reign!"

Sheila took baby Linda down and put her on the potty-chair. The other children wandered off, and J. T. and I sat and smiled at each other over dirty dishes and piled-up chicken bones. He held my hand for a minute, and I thought he was thinking the same thing I was. I was thinking what a wonderful family we have, and how proud he must be to be the father of such a clan. Then he asked softly, "Have you paid the electric bill yet?"

Before I could answer, there was a crash and a yell as baby Linda fell out of the potty-chair and turned it upside down on herself. After settling her down for the night, I answered some letters. One was to a publisher, and I sent him the signed contract which hooked him into publishing my book. Altogether it had been a rare day in heaven. Nothing boring about a day filled with bangs, hems, lectures, platypusses, presidents, devils, ghosts, naughty girls, snakes, potty-chairs and publisher's contracts.

The house creaked and settled for the night and so did I. I'm an ordinary mama, I guess, with ordinary brown hair, ordinary green eyes, the usual number of wrinkles for my age (well, maybe a few more than usual), I'm medium tall, medium fat (hmmm, per haps a little more than medium), and I have medium-sized feet (?). But I'm in a class by myself after all because I'm the mother of four angels, three of them redheads. So I don't feel a bit ordinary. That night after I had popped the corn, Sheila was fervently grateful, "Thanks, Lord, for letting her feel like it."

Sylvia's future medical fingers probed her middle and she remarked, "I'm glad you're here, Mom. We must see about that valve spasm."

Baby Linda whistled in her sleep.

Sandy, my little six-year-old, had hugged me tight and said, "You're beautiful, Mommy. I hope I'm a good Mommy like you some day."

And my husband's sleepy arms encircled me.

Living with angels was heavenly.

Telegram to J. T. Seamands, preaching in Sangli District:

MAHARAJAH IS COMING   BIG FORMAL DINNER AT
RAJAH'S PALACE TOMORROW WE ARE INVITED CAN
YOU COME HOME FOR IT

                                        LOVE   RUTH

Telegram to Mrs. J. T. Seamands, Mission house, Belgaum:

SORRY BUSY IN THE KING'S BUSINESS

                                        LOVE   JAYTEE

I went to the great dinner held at Rani Sahib's palace for her
brother, the Rajah of Baroda, anyway. I hitched a ride in a police
car with the District Superintendent of Police and his wife, who
were good friends of ours.

17

From Tomb To Palace*

Many times we went from our house in Belgaum about 300 miles to Gulbarga, where Mother and Dad Seamands lived and worked as missionaries for the last ten years they were in India. The weather in that part of the country is hotter, more like a desert, with fewer trees and flowers. But the hearts of the Christian people in Gulbarga district are nearly as warm as their country, and they made us feel one with them.

There weren't always Christians in Gulbarga. The story of how Christianity started in that area, and how it progressed is an unusual story. It really started in a tomb—but it jumped to the palace. . . .

It was only three miles, but it took seventy-six long years* to get there, and the man who began the journey never lived to see it completed.

It was the year 1884 that Rev. S. P. Jacob and his wife arrived in the historic city of Gulbarga, the former capital of the Muslim Bahmani Kingdom in the very heart of India. The Jacobs were pioneer missionaries of the Methodist Church to that section of the country. To the people of Gulbarga, Rev. Jacob was a strange man,

*From Tomb To Palace, by J. T. Seamands, reprinted with permission from World Outlook, December 1960.

The Thieves' Tomb. Home of Rev. and Mrs. Jacob, first Methodist missionaries in the Gulbarga, India, area.

with a strange face and a strange religion, so no one was willing to rent them a place to live in the city.

About two miles outside the Gulbarga city limits, there stands all alone on a hilltop, a large stone structure, square-shaped, with a huge dome. This had been built by a very rich Muslim merchant of Gulbarga, and was intended to be the tomb of a famous Muslim saint who lived in the city. But since the merchant had dishonestly acquired most of his wealth, the "saint" refused to grant permission for his body to be buried in the intended tomb. Later, upon his death, he was actually buried in a now-famous mosque in the city. So the mausoleum was left standing unused.

Being the highest spot for miles around, it can be seen from the city. From the train window as one approaches the city, it looks like a trimmed-down castle. Rev. Jacob learned it was unoccupied, and since he and his wife needed a place to stay, they decided to move in. They took their belongings to the top of the hill in bullock carts, and Mrs. Jacob like any housewife, stood in the middle of the 50 x 55-foot one-room tomb and decided which corner should be the living room. It really didn't matter, since all corners were practically the same.

There wasn't even any problem of where to hang clothes in the rainy season. A very high balcony reaching completely around the top of the room about 40 feet up provided the answer. It was a whispering balcony. Even a whisper on one side could be heard perfectly on the other side. Mrs. Jacob simply draped her shirts, skirts, sheets, and sox over the balcony railing when it was raining outside.

Of course, there were problems. Snakes and scorpions and other dangerous creatures sought the coolness of the stone tomb. There were no screen doors. Sometimes rats would chew the strings which help up their mosquito nets. Shops were three miles away. But all in all, it wasn't a bad place to live. They had no rent to pay and nobody disturbed them.

Daily they made visits into the city, walking three miles each way. They talked to the people in the bazaars, in the shops, and in the homes, telling the good news of Christ to any who were willing to listen. Rev. Jacob also made a few trips to the surrounding villages, spreading the good news. On one occasion he went as far as Bidar, another historic city about seventy-five miles away, and preached for several hours in the bazaar. But the people so threatened his life that he had to escape into the darkness.

For nine months they lived in their tomb, and many times they stood at the door on the hilltop, watched the sun set in long, streaked dusty fingers over the city, and prayed that one day Christ would be honored in the midst of the hot, dirty streets below.

After living there for nearly a year, one night the Jacobs were awakened by heavy footsteps, loud talking, and their doors being forced open. A robber gang who had been away on extended exploits had returned to their old hideout—the tomb—only to find it occupied. The Jacobs were forced to run for their lives, leaving everything they owned to the gang of thieves. Where they found shelter, we do not know, but it was in a town some miles distant.

Then came the first ray of light for them amidst the darkness.

One day a high-caste Hindu came to Rev. Jacob, declared his faith in Christ, and asked for Christian baptism. He had heard the good news when Rev. Jacob had preached it one day in the marketplace of the little village of Tinthani, about twenty-five miles from Gulbarga. This Hindu man, Bachanna by name, and his family were baptized and became the first converts of the Methodist Mission in the Nizam's Dominions. At last the seed of the gospel was taking root in the soil. It was a small beginning, but though the church may begin small, it always grows.

Now, over seventy years have come and gone since that first baptismal ceremony. What would a visitor to that section of India find today? He would find hundreds of congregations with a total membership of 150,000 Methodist Christians, living in about 12 ecclesiastical districts, and shepherded by about 500 ordained and supply pastors. He would find four splendid Methodist high schools, seven middle schools, and scores of primary schools, with an enrollment of several thousands of boys and girls.

A visitor would find three well-equipped hospitals, staffed almost entirely by trained Indian Christian personnel. The city of Bidar —where Rev. Jacob was in danger of his life—is now the center of a very thriving mass movement, with almost 35,000 Christians in that one district. There is a fine central church, a hospital, two large boarding schools, and a high school in the city itself. The district superintendent reports that groups from thirty-nine different villages are even today clamoring for baptism. J. T.'s brother, David, was a missionary there for one term.

And what about the city of Gulbarga? It is now a district head-quarters, with a large Christian congregation, and a co-educational high school with 550 students. The mission compound is next door to the summer palace of the Nizam of Hyderabad (the ex-ruler), reputed to be at one time the richest man in the world. He had 400 wives and concubines. Once when a floor in one of the rooms of his palace kept falling down, his building engineers could not keep it repaired. Finally, they asked the Nizam for what purpose the room was used, and he replied that was where he stacked all his gold bricks. After Indian Independence, the Nizam was dethroned like all the Rajahs.

A few years ago, the South India Annual Conference of the Methodist Church was to convene in the city of Gulbarga. My father-in-law, Rev. E. A. Seamands, was the District Superintendent at the time. Realizing that there would not be enough room to house all the ministerial and lay delegates of the conference in the bungalows of the mission compound, my father-in-law requested the new State Government of Hyderabad to permit the conference to use the summer palace of the Nizam. The palace is beautiful and spacious, with a well-kept formal garden all around. It was used only rarely then when His Highness, the Nizam, would visit the city; the rest of the time it was closed. The State Government granted the request, so the Methodists took over the palace for a week. Bishop and Mrs. S. K. Mondol occupied the royal suite of the Nizam. The cabinet meetings were held in the magnificent reception room. The ladies of the WSCS found it hard to concentrate on their business at hand, for they found themselves reclining on soft sofas and satin pillows, surrounded by gold-trimmed pillars, and peering around silken curtains in the rooms where the Nizam's harem used to play.

How could it ever have happened in seventy years? Because Christ is not in the tomb today. Neither can a tomb contain His message. As has been happening since Christ's resurrection, the

Gospel has jumped from tomb to palace—from without the city to the very heart of the city!

That is the story of Christian missions in India. Christ has been taking people out of the tombs of spiritual darkness and death, bringing them back to life, and making them sons and daughters of the King of kings.

December 22nd, 1959, saw the climax of this modern miracle of Christian missions. On that day, a beautiful new church, large enough to accommodate 1000 people was dedicated to the glory of God. It stands right next door to the Nizam's summer palace. Dad Seamands, God's engineer in India, designed it and supervised the building. Built out of cut granite, the church combines elements of Christian, Hindu, and Muslim architecture, and is the talk of the town for its beauty and uniqueness. A red cross shines at night on the top of the church tower. It can be seen for miles around. It can be seen from the thieves' tomb.

If the Jacobs could visit their old hilltop tonight, they would see the ancient tomb dark and deserted. The thieves are long since gone, and nobody whispers in the balcony tonight. They would hear only the swish of wings and see the glow of eyes as owls and bats fly through the abandoned tomb. But the Jacobs' hearts would be glad, for they would hear the Christians singing below, and they would see the cross of Christ glowing in the heart of the dusty city.

18

Alice

Alice Nilijagi is one of our Indian Christian nurses. She was bold enough to give some hostel boys enemas if they complained of stomach ache just so they wouldn't have to go to school.* Few Indian women would have done it, but Alice isn't afraid of anything.

At each conference time we looked forward to Alice's report, for she always had something original. She zestfully does her work, and she loves village people and helps them in so many different ways. In one conference report she noted these unusual cases. (Her own English).

1. A village man brought his third wife with anemia and said, "Madam, treat this wife of mine for her disease and the disobedience to her husband." I asked him about his two previous wives. He said they were wonderful. When I turned to the woman she said, "Yes, my name will be on that list of 'wonderful wives' when he brings his fourth wife to you!"

2. This year most of the women came to the dispensary with one request, "Please help us not to have many children." I wish I would have had some training in family planning to help these sisters of mine. (She was voted to go for this training next year.)

---

*From *Missionary Mama* by Ruth Seamands, New York: Greenwich, 1957.

3. A village head man who is a regular patient to our dispensary and who attended the marriage of our daughter, with his little English introduced me to a new patient and said, "This nurse of ours knows how to match the medicine for the sick, and to patch the young people for marriage.

4. A Muslim woman, mother of twenty-four children, invited me to deliver her twenty-fifth child, in case if she gets.

5. A woman came in and had a tummy upset due to eating a delicious rat curry the previous night, and had a double dose of magsulph to make her all right. (Groans and "ughs" from the conference).

6. A man of 70 years came to the dispensary to find out from the stethoscope as to how long he will live. I told him that I need God's stethoscope to tell that.

7. A man of 65 years who had five daughters came with his wife to our dispensary to get the new injection which will give them a son, but I advised them not to try for son or daughter at this age.

8. A woman came to the antenatal clinic and she was frightened to see the pelvimeter which she had never seen and said, "What are you going to do to me with this big scissors?"

9. A village man, uneducated, was anxious to know about the blood pressure apparatus and he asked me to tell him the use of it. Before I gave any answer, one other uneducated man sitting next to him said, "The first thing the life insurance people ask you about is your blood pressure."

10. In this year I have treated six cases of dog bite, one case of monkey bite and one case of man's bite. Thank God, all are well.

11. A woman who had all four girls was anxious to have a boy and visited my dispensary. As I examined her, I used the new Foetuscope to check up the fetal heart. She was watching me very carefully. Before she left she asked me quietly, "Did the instrument tell you that I will get a boy baby this time? If so, tell my husband, otherwise don't mention anything."

(The previous year Alice had wanted a bicycle in order to visit more village homes, so the mission bought her one. She had never ridden one before, but she learned, wobbling down the road. People see her nurse's uniform, bag, and wobbles, and get out of the way.)

Nurse Alice Nilijagi. Member of South India Annual Conference.

She continued her report, "As the years are passing, the village people are becoming familiar with the mission nurse. The children from distance shout, 'Lady cycle, Lady cycle, come on.' The bicycle is still in good condition after a year's wear, with all my weight (about 150 pounds) with only 4 punctures, fused bulb and loose bell. Still I dream to have a motor scooter some day."

That year she had traveled 405 miles on her bicycle, delivered many babies in village mud huts, treated 2122 patients, visited 338 village homes, gave 187 health talks, and still maintained her buoyant spirit.

For several years we worked together in the same mission station and I learned to love her as my own sister. One day we sat on our front veranda and she told me about some of the village practices and customs surrounding childbirth. I wrote them down just as she told them to me, in English which is not always perfect, but very descriptive.

"Ammah," she began, "how often we read in books and talk among ourselves about the dark ages where people had their evil practices and customs during the delivery times. Though civilization has progressed and education improved, yet we still see such evil practices and customs even today in most of our villages among illiterate people, as well as among people with little education.

"You know I have had the privilege of working among village women for several years during delivery times. I feel very sorry for their ignorance and the cruel ways of treating the newborn child and the mother."

"What do they do that is so bad?" I asked.

"Well, it's like this." She leaned back in my cushioned straw chair and fanned her face with her handkerchief. The day was hot. "A delivery in a village means a great event. The news of delivery time of a woman spreads like a fire in the village. All the women at once rush to the house or the hut where the expectant mother will be living, with their muddy hands, dirty clothes, shabby hair, and dirty feet. One will be quicker than the other in directing the woman to do things—to bear down the child. The house will be full of women all eating the betel leaves and spitting on the floor and chattering about various household business, while waiting to see the newborn child. The doors and windows will be closed to avoid fresh air that they think will kill the baby.

"An old lady is the honorable guest in that house where delivery will take place. The mother will be lying on her mat on the floor. The old lady sits just next to the expectant mother and gives her suggestions about bearing down. Sometimes she will be a mother of a dozen children; sometimes she will be a woman without a single child. Sterility, you know. Sometimes she will be completely blind in sight, and they even choose sometimes a woman who will be too shaky of old age."

"What happens if the woman has complications and cannot deliver?"

"Yes, Ammah, that happens. Many times I was called in the last moment when every effort of such old women fail to deliver babies. My appearance into that particular house will make the village women step out one by one in great fear."

That I could believe. Alice is much larger than the average Indian woman, and her appearance in her white nurse's sari makes her quite overwhelming to small, timid village women. I laughed at the mental picture. "What are some of their strange customs?"

"Well, when the first stage of labor is a little longer than what they expect, then they will order a coconut and some camphor and a measure of ragi (a grain). The person who is ready to deliver baby must take that coconut and seer (a measure) of ragi, place it near the head of the expectant mother; light the camphor, go around the woman thrice, break the coconut and pour its water on her and give some to drink so that she can get good contractions.

"They believe that the goddess 'Kunthie' will be pleased by this worship and come upon the mother and help her to deliver the baby soon. Then the measure of ragi and the coconut will be given to the person who is there to deliver the child. Many times they asked me to do this worship and I said, 'Never!' And thank God I do not allow it when I am there to deliver the baby."

"What do they say when you don't allow them to do this, Alice?"

"They don't do anything, they are afraid of me," she grinned. "I'm too fat and strong." She continued, "When a woman is in second stage of labor, a pot of oil, unsterile of course, will be brought for lubrication and to massage the abdomen. At the same time a special kind of bracelet, made up of five kinds of metals—silver, gold, iron, brass, and copper—will be borrowed and placed on the left arm of the woman who is in labor, so that she will get good contractions and bear down soon. There is such a bracelet in every village. But a particular person must be near the woman to remove the armlet without delay as soon as the head of the baby is out. If not, that bangle will be useless for another woman's delivery. Such bangle was given to my hands once to use for the woman. I kept it in my hand-basin until delivery was over and gave it back to them and advised there is no sense in it. They were disgusted with me.

"An oil lamp will be lit and kept near the woman before the baby arrives. When the baby is out, it must see the light at once; otherwise they believe that baby will be afraid of darkness and think that there is an evil spirit in the darkness which will harm his or her life some day."

My houseboy, a Hindu, came softly out onto the veranda bearing a welcome tea tray. He was wearing his white serving coat with a wide green band, white trousers which I was happy to note were clean, and no shoes. His face gave no indication at all he had overhead any of our conversation. He had made dainty cucumber sandwiches and hot muffins for tea.

"Thank you, Kallappa," I said. "This looks very nice."

He nodded his head and went back inside.

"While we are having tea is a funny time to ask such a question, Alice," I continued, "but I've heard that there is a lot of superstition regarding the baby's cord. Is that true?"

Alice thumped her forehead with her palm in typical Indian fashion. "Ayyo, Ammah, how many superstitions there are about the cord! As soon as the child comes out, the old women will get together and watch the neck and shoulder of the baby, to see whether the cord is around the neck or shoulder. If it is around the neck, they believe that the uncle of the newborn (mother's brother) will face a great difficulty in life. If the cord is across the shoulders, the midwife will face the difficulty in life. So to avoid risk for the uncle, a coconut will be made into two pieces, and in one piece the old lady of the house will pour castor oil and ask the young and old uncles of the house to see their faces in the oil. If they say they can see, the old lady will be very happy. Negative answer will upset her.

"Once I delivered a baby with cord around the neck. When they were following the same custom, I peeped in the oil and said, 'I don't see anything in the oil, no face, no head.' So the old woman got disgusted and said I needed high-power glasses!

"If the cord is across the shoulder then a chicken will be given to the person who delivers the baby. She should cut the chicken, cook it and eat it by herself. When such was given to me I said, 'Please cut it and make nice curry, and feed the mother who needs a lot of nourishment.'

"When the baby arrives they watch the color of the baby very closely. If they see any slight blue color, then they will at once give the orders to the man or woman to run to the dhoby's house (house of the man who washes the clothes) and get a glass of donkey milk from the dhoby's donkey, and make the newborn child drink it. It is also their belief that this milk will give long life to the baby.

"If the cord has many twists, then they will say, 'Too many children will be born.' If the twists are big and black, they believe these are going to be boys; if the cord-twists are thin and red, then they will be girls. One woman of whom I know had a baby three years ago and was told by her midwife that she will have some more boys, whereas she has none. They believe if they cut the cord as soon as the baby is born, or after some time, the placenta will go up into the chest cavity and stick there, so they are not supposed to cut cord until the placenta is out.

"When the third stage is over, the placenta will be put into a mud pot with three pieces of betel leaves and betel nuts and must be buried deep in the earth. If not, an evil spirit will be after that family and give trouble in many ways. If a dog sees the placenta, they believe the mother will suffer from having no milk to feed the baby."

She helped herself to another cucumber sandwich and held out her cup for more tea. The great leaves of the mighty banyan trees which surrounded the mission house, rustled in the slight breeze. Sunlight filtered through these leaves onto the grassy area which was the children's playground, and munchings could be heard from the small herd of buffalos grazing on our compound. It was so peaceful there—hard to believe that just a few miles away in hundreds of villages such superstitious practices "walked" with the birth of every baby.

"When the oil bath for the baby is over, the midwife is asked to *brand* the child with a hot needle or bracelet piece," she continued. "The . . ."

I jumped and my teacup rattled in the saucer. "Brand the child!" I exclaimed.

"Yes, Ammah, *brand* the child with a hot needle or bracelet piece. The lucky number is nine, so five brandings are done around the umbilicus, and two on each side of the chest."

"Oh, Alice, I've seen scars on the stomachs of our hostel children, and never knew what caused them. How can they do that to a tiny baby?"

"Because they believe that each branding will cure ten diseases of the newborn child. It is very bad. The dressing for the branding then is saffron powder, garlic, salt, and castor oil. It is pathetic to see the suffering of the child when dressing is done. How often they get these things ready for me to brand the child! I always tell them that I will brand the woman first who got the things ready for it. I am very hard on them for such cruel deeds in my medical practice.

"Suppose a woman has lost all her babies right after birth, and one particular child is saved from danger. Then a ring will be made of gold and one pearl. It must be placed in the nose or the left ear. It is very painful to the child as the midwife pokes the nose or the ear. They believe this ring will save the child from death."

"I suppose that's why we sometimes see a boy with a pierced ear?"

"No doubt that is the reason."

"Sometimes when the placenta takes some time to be expelled," she continued, "the village people will get very excited, and they give dirty, false hair to the mother to chew. When she starts chewing, she will feel nauseated and vomit. Thus, the placenta will be expelled due to pressure. If this fails, they will mix salt and soot in cold water to give to the woman to drink. Again, when she feels like vomiting, the placenta will perhaps be expelled. Sometimes a hard massage is done on the abdomen. Sometimes they walk on the woman's back with their bare feet."

I shuddered, thinking how if there ever was a time when a woman felt less like having somebody walk on her back—

"The dried cord that falls from the baby is very precious to the village people. Sometimes they tie it to the cradle for three months to avoid evil spirits at night. Sometimes they fix it in a silver armlet and wear to avoid evil spirits attacks. Sometimes they bury it in a banana or a cooked grain ball and give it to the woman who does not have any children. She will swallow this in the morning before she takes any food. It is the belief of the village women that if a woman swallows such a cord, she will have children in the future."

Alice grinned as I gagged on my sandwich. "If it took that to have kids, I'm afraid I'd go my whole life without them! What happens if the woman dies in childbirth?"

"When a woman dies during delivery time and before the baby is born, the husband must cut open her abdomen with a glass piece or broken bracelet, take out the baby and leave both bodies at the graveyard. If a doctor is available, the husband will ask him to open his wife's abdomen with his knife. If not, the husband must do this. Then he must put a cloth on his head and leave his home and his village and go and wander wherever he likes for three months. Then he comes back to the village, shaves himself, must take holy bath and visit the temple, then come back to his house."

We sat, thinking over what she had just told me. "I really admire you, Alice, for your work delivering babies in villages and fighting such beliefs."

"Ammah, I've tried to teach them the proper way to deliver a baby. I talk to them about nourishing food, fresh air, and mostly the cleanliness which is very badly needed in the villages. It is terrible for mothers to deliver in village homes in such dirt. They are given no nourishing food or even a drink of water during many hours of pain, and they suffer in the heat with no fresh air at all. But they are so slow to understand. It will take long time to teach them about the real God, and to forget about evil spirits. I always testify for my Lord when I work in villages. Pray for me, Ammah," she said, balancing her bulk on her frail, English bicycle. She put her nurse's kit in the basket and waved.

"I wish India had ten thousand Alices to do just what you're doing," I called after her as her bicycle weaved and wobbled down the brick-red driveway toward her village clinic.

19

To Sea in a Ship

It was time for our furlough, and we had to pack during May, one of the hottest months of the year in India. Many people came to tell us goodbye, and urged us to hurry back. We'd been showered with farewell dinners and garlands and speeches of appreciation. I wanted to go home to America, but it made me sad to leave all the friends with whom we'd worked and loved so long.

One day my heart almost broke. The elderly lady from the village who had leprosy on her leg came in. She had walked the ten miles into town to tell us good-bye. She never openly confessed that she was a Christian, but we were sure she was a believer in Christ. When she came into our house that day, she threw herself down at J. T.'s and my feet. We tried to get her to stand up, but she took hold of our feet and wept. She said, "Sahib, don't go away! Mem-Sahib, don't go away! When you leave us the light will go out. The light will go out."

Both of us wept too. We love that old lady. Perhaps we are the only people who had shown her any love in a long time.

But I could hardly wait to see America again. Five years is a long time to be away from one's country. I was homesick for country, for relatives and friends too. I am incurably patriotic; no one can imagine what happens inside me when I see an American flag. I choke and blink and wonder whether all the people who have lived in America for all their lives really appreciate their wonderful land. The American flag is the most beautiful in the whole world!

It seems we are destined never to have a calm voyage anywhere.

At last the time for our furlough arrived, and we were on the docks at Bombay early in the morning. Sylvia, now graduated from high school, had been twelve when she last saw America. Sheila, now thirteen, had been only eight. Sandy, now nine, had just celebrated her fourth birthday at Grandma Childers' house the day before we left for India five years before; and Linda wasn't even thought of. We were all so excited we'd hardly slept the night before in the hotel room in Bombay.

The next day at the docks we lined up, with about fifteen pieces of hand luggage, had our passports and health papers checked, and after a three hour wait were waved onto the ship.

I picked up as many things as I could carry, looked around to see if all the kids were following, and told them to each take what they could handle. J. T. was walking on ahead with two heavy suitcases. Linda, two years old, had her own little private potty-chair. It was an Indian chair of woven bamboo, and we took it wherever we went for Linda was afraid of the large toilets. I thought I might have trouble with her in the unfamiliar atmosphere of the ship if I didn't have her own little chair. The easiest way to carry it, as far as I could see, was to put it in a pillow case. I know that nobody travels like that in America, but in India we take everything with us all the time, so it didn't bother me at all.

That morning when I told the kids each to take what they could carry, Linda immediately grabbed the pillow case containing her potty-chair, threw it over her shoulder and followed J. T., mimicking his long strides, for about a quarter of a mile down the dock to the gangplank. She looked like an animated doll with her red curly hair, freckled face and frilly yellow dress. The pillow case was big, and with her every step, the chair thumped on the docks behind her. Everyone who was lined up to get on board was watching her and laughing. Sylvia and Sheila and I were very amused and offered to carry her chair, but she didn't want help from anyone.

As soon as we were aboard ship, we heard rumors of a shipping strike on all Italian lines, but we didn't think much about it. We had a fancy turkey dinner that night, watched the moon come up over the Arabian sea, and went to bed. Early the next morning we were awakened by stillness. One gets used to the hum of the ship's engines and vibrations all the time, so immediately it is stopped, everyone wants to see why.

We got up and dressed and went to the dining room for breakfast. Nobody there; no lights on; no activity. No breakfast. There was a sign posted on the bulletin board: "We wish to inform the passengers on this ship that the entire crew is on strike."

We were bewildered. We were on a silent ship in Karachi harbor, not able to get off, and not knowing what to do. The rest of the family dejectedly went back to our cabin thinking that somebody would get busy cooking soon. I wasn't so optimistic, so I searched the buffet there in the dining room, helped myself to three half-bottles of ketchup and half a box of crackers I found. We had ketchup and crackers for breakfast.

About ten o'clock, Linda started to complain that she was hungry and wanted some warm tea or milk or something. I was beginning to get a little huffy about the whole hungry situation, so I marched myself back to the dining room. Still nobody there. I followed my nose out to the ship's kitchen, and there was the whole kitchen crew, sitting around long, white tables drinking coffee and eating fragrant hot bread. My temperature rose at the sight.

I walked straight up to the dining room steward and asked him in a controlled voice, "Won't you please ask your men to get some breakfast, at least for the children? They are so hungry."

He shook his head. "Sorry, Madam, no."

My temper flared. "You and your crew can sit here guzzling

coffee and starve your adult passengers to death if you want to, but please do something for the children. There are lots of hungry children crying up and down the halls."

He shrugged and said, "Sorry, Madam, we *feel* for the children, but we can't break strike."

That did it. I looked at those ten or fifteen big fat fellows drinking and eating, and said with scorn, "Yes, I *bet* you all feel for the poor little children! You just *look* like you do. I bet you are even crying in that coffee. All right, then, if you aren't going to do any work, please give me the keys to the cupboards and all of you get out of here. I'll go get some women and we will cook some food for our children. We aren't helpless. We're not on strike!"

He shrugged again and said, "Sorry, Madam, I can't do that."

Then I got so mad my stomach hurt and I yelled at him, "You'd just better do it!" Then I started to cry and that made me madder than ever. I sniffed and shouted, "I'm going upstairs and round the women up, and I'm coming down here with every mother on this ship, and if you don't give our children something to eat, we are really going to wreck this kitchen! We *will not* sit here, unable to get off this ship and see our children hungry and crying, with all that food which we have paid for locked up and the keys in your pocket. You won't even have any pocket! Now you'd better think about that, for I mean it!" And I stamped, I really stamped, out of that door and started down the hall knocking on doors getting mothers together.

I'm sure he realized I meant business, and he must have called an emergency session of the kitchen crew, for within just a few minutes a room steward ran down the hall after me and said, "Madam, I've been sent to tell you there will be milk and cookies for the children in the dining room in ten minutes. Please have some mothers come in and help us serve it."

The other mothers and I grimly marched all our children into the dining room—between two and three hundred of them—and helped the stewards give out milk and cookies. That satisfied the children at least for a time.

Then there was an announcement made over the loud speakers to the effect that at twelve o'clock there would be buses leaving the docks for downtown Karachi, about ten miles away, and the passengers could go off and have lunch there. By this time, the temperature outside was about 115 degrees in the shade, and the children were exhausted from the excitement of the morning. They were not hungry then anyway, so Sheila, Sandy, and Linda all said they would stay on the ship. For Sylvia, J. T., and me, the first ketchup and crackers had long since been digested, and I thought I couldn't face another ketchup bottle. We said we'd go, and promised to bring something from town for the children.

The three of us went down the gangplank and were waiting on the Karachi dock for the buses when another announcement from the ship came over the loudspeaker. "Since we are on strike here, we cannot remain at this dock. We will be in another position when you return." The ship was already beginning to move!

I suddenly became panicky, remembering our three children in our cabin. I realized they would look out the porthole, see the ship moving and think it was going off without Mother, Daddy, and Sylvia, and they would be scared to death. I started running toward the ship yelling at J. T. over my shoulder, "I've got to get back on board and stay with the kids!"

He called, "Don't go!" and tried to catch me, for the ship was moving. But it hadn't moved far yet; the gangplank was only about a foot or so away from the dock, and I always was a good jumper. So jump I did. I jumped off the dock, grabbed the gangplank, and crawled up as they were drawing it up. One of the sailors at the top hauled me on board by the back of my dress and said, "Lady, you sure took a chance that time!"

I looked over the side at the ever-widening water, and down at

J. T.'s and Sylvia's look of horror and then started to shake. I muttered to the sailor's bewilderment, "Back to the ketchup bottle for me!"

He shrugged, "Americano!"

The next day the passengers got together in the big lounge and elected a committee of four men and one woman to consult with the Captain about either getting us off this ship or giving us the services we had already paid for. They elected me as that one woman. They said it was because of the heroic way I had, unarmed and single-handed, stood up to the kitchen crew the day before. I hadn't even thought about being heroic. It's just that when I get good and mad, people better get out of my way.

So the five of us called on the Captain. He said he felt sorry for us, but couldn't do a thing, as his whole crew was on strike. He would negotiate with his home office by telephone, and try to get them to charter planes for us. They couldn't call on other Italian ships, for the whole Italian fleet was on strike.

Meanwhile, we stayed for a week on that ship, which got dirtier and stinkier by the day. There wasn't a floor swept, not a bed made, not a bathroom washed, not a clean towel or sheet given, not a roll of toilet paper given out by a crew member. The passengers did all those things for themselves. We had limited access to the cleaning supplies and toilet paper. Garbage from the crew's meals lay on the deck (they weren't allowed to throw it overboard) and the crew sat in the middle of it with their feet up, and had a noisy alcoholic rest. It was the worst week we'd ever seen.

Every day, buses took us three times a day ten miles into Karachi for our meals. It must have cost the ship-owners a fortune. Then the United States Embassy came to the rescue of the Americans on board. They came on and gave us permission to buy American candy, condensed milk, canned meat, kleenex, toilet paper, and things like that from the American PX. The only hitch was, we had to order it a day in advance, then the next day line up for delivery at twelve noon. There was always a long line on the dock, standing right in the sun, in June in Karachi, with the thermometer nearly spewing out its top. It was awful. People fainted right in the line. But we did get some American food which we could eat cold in the cabins. The trips to town through the heat three times a day in those slow buses were utterly exhausting, and half the time the children refused to go. They'd rather be hungry, they said.

Then we had wonderful news. Planes were chartered to go to Europe, and three of us were to go out on the first plane at midnight. The other three were to follow on the next plane the next day. We decided that I should go on the first plane with the two smallest children. We had to leave most of our luggage on the ship, however, and could take only one piece of luggage each. I took a suitcase for each of us; Linda chose, guess what? Of course, her pillow case and potty-chair. We were off.

The flight to Zurich, Switzerland, was beautiful. After suffering in that Karachi heat, Switzerland looked like heaven. We kept exclaiming about the green grass, the cool refreshing air, flowers in the windows, and the cleanliness of the country. Living in India for five years at a stretch, we had forgotten how clean some countries are.

And the food! We'd been on half diet for a week, and our stomachs were shrunk. I ordered three dinners for us, and we had enough to feed ten people. The next meal I ordered just one complete dinner, and it was more than enough for the three of us.

Twenty-four hours later the other three family members arrived and we had a heavenly stop on our journey to America.

20

Adjustments

The children adjusted to America as if it were the easiest thing in the world, but the language problem baffled Linda. Having been taken care of most of the time in India by a nurse maid who spoke no English, she was very proficient in the Kanarese language, and didn't speak English at all. She understood it perfectly when we spoke to her, but she answered us in Kanarese. She said it was easier. It was so funny to watch her play with a little boy on our street. She would shout at him in Kanarese and he'd just go on with what he was doing and pay no attention to her at all. She'd get very angry. But her friend did pick up some of her words. He began calling a bug "poochie," a blanket "cumberlie," and saying "ba" for come, and "hogu" for go. But mostly he didn't understand Linda.

One day it seemed to dawn on her that people weren't paying any attention to her if she spoke Kanarese, so she decided to try English. She swung into it easily, for she had a perfect English vocabulary all stored up in that red-head of hers. However, her words sometimes came out in an Indian sequence. Whereas in English we say, "I am going to town today," Linda said it, "To town going today I am." And for "Give me my blanket," she said, "My blanket, give." But after a while her English improved, though with a slight British accent. We wondered what her accent would be like when it got mixed up with Kentucky.

I've mentioned before how forgetful J. T. is. Once he left me dressed and ready to go to a dinner at the Rajah's palace—just forgot me completely and started off in the jeep. Then the children told me a story which he'd tried to keep secret for some time.

It seems that once he took them camping down to Jog Falls in India. They had their picnic lunch, and J. T. washed the dishes in the wash basin. As he threw the dishwater away down the toilet, he heard a terrible clatter. He had thrown away the silverware too. I never saw anyone drawing silverware out of a toilet. "Fascinating," the children said.

America didn't change him. My wonderful husband is still forgetful, and once in a while he gets his tongue twisted too. I think there will be many people in Kansas City who will remember him for a long time. He had a week's series of meetings there, and one night to a packed auditorium he was preaching on the Christian home. J. T. first told the wives how they should love and honor their husbands, and not spend too much money. Then he started on the husbands. He told them to show their wives more affection and consideration. He said among other things, "Surprise your wife tomorrow. When you go home from work, take her a box of chocolates. And she will be so surprised you'd better take her a bottle of"—he meant to say "smelling salts because she might faint" but got his tongue twisted and said "epsom salts"—and that is as far as he got because the audience exploded. Then he realized what he'd said and got so tickled he just had to stop preaching, hang on to the pulpit, and laugh. It was bedlam for at least fifteen minutes while people held their stomachs and laughed. Oh well, even great men do make mistakes.

My husband works quite closely with Dr. E. Stanley Jones. One day he was telling Dr. Jones about this incident in Kansas City, so E. Stanley told him one mistake he had made. In a meeting which was about to finish, Dr. Jones was preaching and was thinking ahead about how to end the service by making an appeal for decisions for Christ. He first thought, "I'll ask them if they want to decide for Christ to put up their hands," then his second thought was, "No, I'll ask them to stand to their feet."

Well, he got his words confused and what he *said* was, "All of you who want this blessing, put up your feet!"

One old lady sitting on the front row look surprised and groaned, "Lord, help us!"

So two great men, E. Stanley Jones, and J. T. Seamands are both human after all.

21

Indian Dinner for the Bachelor

A good friend in America asked me how she could hook a wary bachelor. This is what I wrote to her:

Say you've snagged a bachelor who's been here and there. Say he's wined you and dined you in fancy French, earthy Italian, and ching-chung restaurants, so you know he savors foreign foods. Scoot way out (on that limb) and invite him to an Indian dinner at your apartment.

Choose a day when you will have at least an afternoon to slave over the stove. Well, you want him, don't you? He'll luxuriate in your dinner, and you know the old saying about hearts and stomachs and routes.

You could buy a special dress for the occasion, made from sari silk, put a flower in your hair and a *bottu* in the middle of your forehead with your lipstick, but with a dinner like this, don't be surprised if he doesn't flip over what you're wearing. Those tantalizing aromas will meet him at the door and he'll succumb to the siege of the genius who produced it. Game? Okay, it's your wedding—

MENU: Yellow rice, chicken curry, tomato chutney, pineapple chutney, puris, iced tea, maple syrup.

What to buy the day before:
2 full chicken breasts, halved; 4 pieces (one for you)
2 pkgs. frozen coconut
1 small can tomato puree (8 oz. size)
1 box rice (not the quick variety)
Spices: whole cloves, stick cinnamon, turmeric powder, curry powder,
        whole cardamon (or ground cardamon if you can't obtain
        the whole), ground ginger, Accent (monosodium glutamate)
small clove garlic (can omit if you don't like the lingering melody)

4 medium-sized onions	1 small can crushed pineapple
3 medium-sized potatoes	1 tomato (large)
small pkg. whole-wheat flour	handful seedless raisins
cooking oil	1 small pkg. cashew nuts
a little milk	2 eggs
2 bananas	1 pkg. sour cream
small bottle maple syrup	stick of butter or margerine
	small pkg. white flour

If you're startled at this grocery bill, remember the eight-dollar steaks he fed you.

Better start this about three o'clock.

First: *the rice.* Put six cups boiling water in a pan, add the two packages frozen coconut. Let stand about 15 minutes over heat, and bring to another boil without letting it boil over. Remove from heat and strain water off into another saucepan. Keep the water, throw coconut away.

In a pan put 2 cups long-grained rice, 4 cups coconut water, 1 tablespoon salt, 2 sticks cinnamon, about 6 whole cloves, 3 cardamon, and just enough turmeric powder to make rice a light yellow color, ½ stick butter. Let mixture come to a boil, turn down heat to low and put on lid. Simmer about 25 minutes, stirring occasionally with a *cooking fork* so as not to mash the rice.

While rice is simmering, start the curry.

Into a large, heavy kettle, put 3 onions cut into small pieces, and one minced garlic clove (if you're game). Add ⅓ cup cooking oil. Stir and cook onions on medium heat until about half done. (About 10 minutes).

Into onions put 1½ heaping tablespoons curry powder (don't inhale now), about 6 whole cloves, 2 sticks cinnamon, 3 cardamon (or use a small pinch of ground cardamon), a teaspoon ground ginger, 1 teaspoon Accent. Stir. Now put in well-salted pieces of raw chicken. Stir to coat chicken with onion mixture. Add the can of tomato puree and about 2 cups coconut water. Cover, turn down heat and cook on low until chicken is about half done. Then add 3 medium-sized potatoes, cut in eighths. Continue cooking until potatoes are done, adding plain water if more juice is desired. Turn off heat. Waiting doesn't hurt this; it only enhances flavor.

Done all that? Have a cup of coffee.

While the curry is cooking, if the rice has cooked 25 minutes, put the *uncovered* pan of rice in an oven set at lukewarm (about 150 degrees). Leave the rice in there until time to eat—and fluff it with a fork every half hour. Indian curry abhors sticky rice.

Got this far? Good sailing, don't sink now. Let's make the puris (pronounced poorie) :

Mix ½ cup whole wheat flour, ½ cup white flour, pinch salt in a bowl. Add about 1 tablespoon cooking oil and just enough milk to make a slightly sticky ball of dough. Knead this on floured board for a few minutes. Roll it and pound it and knuckle-knead it. Then cover it with damp cloth and let it rest.

But *you* don't. Now you make the tomato chutney. Easy. Cut the tomato and onion in small, small pieces. Add a pinch of salt, a couple of sprinklings of Accent, and a big heaping tablespoon or two of sour cream. Mix well and set covered in refrigerator until dinner is on the table. Easy, huh?

Time to make pineapple chutney. Strain juice off the crushed pineapple, and mix pineapple with 2 bananas cut in small pieces.

Indians like something sweet and something hot together, you know.

Boil two eggs about 7 minutes. Must be hard-boiled. Then peel and set aside.

Have you been fluffing your rice? Then knead your dough for another 2 minutes. Cover again. Taste the curry to see if salt is sufficient.

Go set the table. Candles too. Indians eat with their fingers, but if you'd rather not, put out your best silver.

Curry needs a cool drink. Make the iced tea now. Sweeten it while it's still hot. Much better.

Get your rolling pin. Pinch off the dough into balls somewhat smaller than golf balls. Remember your jack-ball when you were little? About like that. Roll each one out flat and thin. Don't stack or they'll stick.

Into a deep fat fryer or electric skillet put about 4 inches of cooking oil. Heat to very hot; electric skillet on highest point, or stove on high. First throw in handful of cashew nuts, and take out immediately with slotted spoon or strainer. Do same with handful of raisins. Quick now, or they'll burn. Then keep them warm in your oven with the rice.

Now fry the puris, one at a time. Drop them into the very hot fat, spooning oil on top. Cook about ½ minute on each side, or to very light brown. These should puff up and be hollow in the middle. If they don't, don't fret. My Indian cook's often didn't either—they're good anyway. Now stand the puris on their sides in a long, high-sided pan and keep them warm in the oven; UN-COVERED, or they'll get tough.

Change your dress, powder your nose. Add whatever falsies you intend to. Was that the door bell? Make him comfortable, and turn on fire under curry. Heat just to boiling now; don't cook any more.

Arrange yellow rice on a platter, mounded up. Sprinkle your raisins and cashews over top, and dot with sliced hard-boiled eggs.

Pour the tea, dish up the curry, and don't forget your two chutneys. You won't have to call him, he's probably already at the table.

Bring out the puris as needed—warm from the oven. These are to be eaten with the curry and rice, but finish up the last one with some maple syrup. That'll really orbit him, and you won't need dessert. He couldn't hold it anyway.

I bet you get him.

If anybody else reads this and you've already got him and kids too, this recipe can be doubled or tripled or proportioned for big crowds. Any way you do it, you're a winner.

22

Missionary Career Over?

Our year of furlough was at an end and we were packing to go back to India, but we were very concerned about Sandy. She began to have a fever every afternoon, she had no energy to go out and play, and she could hardly eat anything. She got thinner and more listless all the time. We wondered if she didn't want to leave America to go back to India, but she said she did. Through the whole summer she seemed to become weaker.

We had already sent Sheila back to India by plane in June because that was when her school year started in Kodaikanal. She would not be with us again until the last of October when her school let out for the long holiday.

Toward the end of the summer Sandy's illness was diagnosed as histoplasmosis, a disease which on the x-ray looks like tuberculosis, but which does not respond to tuberculosis treatment. As soon as our mission board heard what the trouble was, they refused to give us a medical okay to return to India, because it is difficult to recover from a lung ailment in the tropics. Of course we were upset and also concerned about Sheila in India without any of the rest of her family. It took us three days to reach her by telephone (they had finally been able to get telephone service to the top of that mountain) to tell her the situation. At the end of October, she flew back to America. Sylvia said, "Boy, I wouldn't mind getting a trip around the world by myself at the age of fourteen!"

We prayed much about what our future should be, for we had expected to be missionaries in India until retirement age. We both knew our future was in God's hands, and now it seemed He was leading us in another direction.

J. T. had been offered a job before, to become the professor of missions at Asbury Theological Seminary in Kentucky. He had refused because we felt our place was in India. Now the offer came again and he accepted it, for he could still, in a sense, be a missionary. Three quarters of the year he is a professor, and the fourth quarter he travels to different mission fields of the world, studying problems and people, methods, and indigenous churches. So he is very well informed as to the worldwide mission situation.

Usually I stay in America when J. T. takes his mission tours, but a year or so ago I went back to India with him. How different it is to be a visitor to India instead of living there! Now I've seen India from both kinds of eyes. I feel sorry for tourists who get at best only a superficial look at India. How can they possibly understand the Indian mind in simply flying from one city to another, staying in fine suites in leading hotels, and chatting in English with a few people? India's problems are deep and not easily understood by Westerners, especially since so many of her problems have origins in the Hindu religion.

The reverence for all life—especially for cows, monkeys and snakes—has never been understood by the West. We don't understand why they do not have a democracy just like ours. We simply cannot see why—with trying a little harder—they couldn't cut down their birth rate and step up their food production. And a most difficult thing for us to comprehend is why village people use all the cow manure as fuel with which to cook their food, and as a coating on the floors of their village homes, instead of putting it back on the fields as fertilizer.

No prior ideas or movies could possibly prepare a visitor to India for the shocking reality of the filth, deprivation, overcrowded masses and scarcity of food and shelter.

And of couse, India does not understand us either.

When we went back as visitors, Gene Moore (an evangelistic singer with a most angelic tenor voice) went with us. We traveled and worked together for a month and we could never have found a more companionable co-worker. I just sat back and watched Gene "take in" India. Of course, I felt immediately at home, but Gene couldn't relax. There was simply too much for him to see.

He sat up on the edge of the seat in the tiny, crowded taxi, wiping sweat from his face, sure we'd be dead the next minute. We sped through teeming streets with unbelievable daredevil taxi drivers, darting and dodging through thousands of carts, scooters, cows, bullocks, bicycles, people carrying luggage on their heads and walking in the middle of the road. One taxi driver we had was a Sikh, his long, curly hair done up in a knot under a dirty white turban. His car was 15 years old, and burning oil furiously. The floorboards were very loose, so the oil fumes kept coming up in Gene's face. We doubted whether it would ever get us across town, but it did, sputtering protest and shuddering every time the clutch was let out.

We had traveled so much that we hadn't been able to lie down or really sleep from Monday night until Thursday night. By that time I was keyed up higher than that topknot under the Sikh's turban. Also, my feet were swollen, and I didn't dare take my shoes off until we arrived at the place where we were spending the first night—I'd never have been able to get them back on again.

Our first night we stayed with some missionary friends in New Delhi. What a relief to get our shoes off, have dinner, and fall into bed! I thought I could sleep through anything, but that was before the chowkidar came on duty at 9:30. His heavy shoes must have been three sizes too large for him, with heavy steel plates where the heels should have been. And, as if his shoes didn't make enough noise, his stick completed the job. He clonked round and round the house all night long, with his shoes and stick, to let us know he wasn't sleeping and would protect the compound from robbers. Every half hour he gave a loud cough. Then at 3 A.M., the thieving and witching hour, he coughed louder than before, then broke into a song in a low and mournful key—a nasal moan through which nobody could sleep. It was designed to wake us all up and tell us he was on the job. In the middle of putting my pillow over my ears, I heard Gene laughing in the next room. Laughing! at 3 A.M. when we hadn't slept for four nights!

Gene's humor was still in good form even after such a night. He was dazzled by the Taj Mahal, and he was ignited by the lunch. He said the mutton curry was like eating a soft blowtorch—lighted, of course.

The incredibility of India is its contrasts. Between the airport and Bombay city are some of the worst slums in the world; old shacks made out of cans and rags, backwater in every yard about six inches deep; naked babies, dogs, buffalos all in the water; women washing clothes in the same water, and even brushing their teeth there. We saw all this within a few miles of the beautiful skyline of Marine Drive. And within a few hours we were whisked to a National Defense Academy, with its magnificent buildings, swimming pool, fine homes, and everything spotlessly clean.

India has her problems with sexual deviates, as all countries do. We saw a group of people sitting on the ground alongside the street in Bombay. They had very obvious male faces, but long hair, and they wore saris—a low-looking class of people, unkempt and dirty. "They are eunuch homosexuals," our host (a policeman) said.

"Those words sound mutually exclusive. How can they do anything if they are eunuchs?"

He answered, "In the homosexual business they don't really do anything. They are just the passive partners."

I asked if they were man-made eunuchs or God-made. He said, "man-made."

We started to a sari shop, a fine one where one can examine hundreds of very expensive pure silk saris, with gold and silver woven in. We were almost there when we got into a traffic jam, and finally had to get out of the taxi and walk. The jam involved two huge trucks (lorries, in India) trying to pass each other in a narrow lane. Behind each truck were different traffic hazards including two cars, a buffalo, a goat, a man pulling a foot-pedal sewing machine tied onto a flat two-wheeled cart, a bullock cart, and a four-wheeled cart full of knick-knacks for sale. We pushed our way through the throng; I steadied myself on the sewing machine, slid by the truck, and smelled the goat before finding a clear passage and darting into the sari shop.

One person whom I longed to see in India was Alice. For the past year she had been working in a Tibetan refugee camp. When the Chinese invaded Tibet a few years ago, and began slaughtering many Tibetans, especially Buddhist priests, many thousands began the dangerous trek into India, across the Himalayas. They brought only what they could carry on their backs. After selling what they had brought, they were destitute, so the Indian government provided refugee camps for them in various parts of India. The National Christian Council sent in nurses to help. Alice was one. Knowing that her story about the Tibetans would be fascinating, I was anxious to hear it. Over cups of strong tea, laced with boiled buffalo milk and sugar, and plates of curry puffs (curried meat in small half-moon shaped pies) and cookies, she told me about her year in the refugee camp. I was full of questions about the Tibetan people, for they had always had a fascination for me. Tibet had always been a closed land as far as missionaries and most visitors were concerned.

Alice sipped her tea and began: "There were only three of us in charge: the Superintendent and her husband, both Anglo-Indians, and myself. The road into the camp is narrow. There was thick jungle around these camps when we first arrived, but with the help of the government the jungles are cleared now and the beautiful land is cultivated by the refugees.

"We started our New Year with simple rice and curry, had our New Year's service in the creche building itself, with the roof only half on. The moon and stars were looking at us three when we had our watch-night service at midnight. No pastor, no congregation, no instruments to hear. We sang with sore throats due to heavy mist, and praised God for taking us safely to those camps.

"Hundreds of refugees rushed to greet us when we arrived. I was the first Indian woman wearing a sari and blouse to come to live amidst them to work. Their narrow eyes and fat faces with grinning expression greeted us, and the thick dirt on their palms was a shock to our hands as we shook hands.

"There are nearly three thousand refugees in all these camps, put up within the radius of six miles. The houses are made with bamboo, mud, and tiles. Each house (the size of your living room, Ammah) gives shelter to five married families. These five families live together in this single house with their children, cattle, chickens, and pigs."

"How in the world do they get along like that?"

Alice grinned. "Well, you know the old proverb 'two women cannot live under one roof' is common here in these refugee houses also. They start fighting with one another, then tell their men they can't stand each other's families, so they go out and put up a hut on their land. Thus, we see small huts in the fields here and there. Our government gave each family one acre of land for cultivation, and one bull to plough the land. Usually all five families put their five acres together and join their five bulls and cultivate the land.

"Among these three thousand refugees there are two hundred Lamas, Buddhist priests. These Lamas live in the fourth camp. There are two kinds of priests. The yellow-cap Lamas never marry, but live as priests, always doing puja (worship). They shave their heads and dress in long, red skirts with yellow jackets. The other group marry and live with their families, but they are not as holy as the others! They are not as holy to the Tibetans because they live as others."

I was glad to see Alice hadn't lost an ounce of her zest for life. The curry puff tasted wonderful; the strong, sweet tea was just right. I chewed a curry puff and asked, "What do the Tibetans eat?"

"Well, they are wheat eaters and meat eaters also. They eat much more than we eat. They prepare their wheat bread with high doses of baking soda. The children chew on that bread almost ten hours in a day. They call it 'Suddu.' Fried wheat flour is mixed with Tibetan tea and is enjoyed by these people. 'Logo Momma,' wheat balls which look like sponge cakes, are very popular among them for every meal. They like rice too. Pork is their favorite food but they never boil it enough, so they suffer with tapeworms. Dhall, (split peas) and vegetables are used little. Though they grow ragi (a grain) they don't prepare it as a food, but as an intoxicating liquor to drink. They are very fond of it. Everybody, young or old, enjoys drinking. Sometimes they throw boiled ragi to the pigs and the pigs get drunk and go reeling and grunting over the ground!

"The Tibetans seem to need a lot of food for every meal. I have actually seen my creche ayahs (nursemaids) eating three or four breads, very thick and big as a plate, with vegetables and tea. Whereas we Indian women will eat one and a half breads for a full meal, they take twice that much."

"I've heard about the Tibetan tea. Is it good?"

"Ayyo, their tea is ghastly! It's red, extremely strong tea with a lump of salt and yak butter. I will never forget the day of my arrival. They made me drink six or seven cups of their tea which kept me with nausea for a whole day. I cannot think of that tea when I am in sick bed. It gives me the idea of epsom salts. Ugh!

And they eat their meat even when there are maggots in it. A few people eat fish and frogs because mutton is very costly. They use it during festival times. Now I have taught them to prepare ragi balls and porridge for their meals."

"It's probably just as well I never got to visit Tibet, after hearing about that food."

"Oh, Ammah, you're a good cook; you'd hate that food."

"What crops do they grow on that acre of land?"

"This cleared land is very fertile. Each family grows the crops according to its own desire. Potatoes, tobacco, rice, ragi, cotton, and dhall are the common crops we see. The men and women walk to the fields in the morning with their teakettles and work there until the evening. They carry their babies on their backs while they work. If babies go to sleep the mothers will put them under the bushes for rest."

"How about their clothes?"

Alice thumped her head. "Their clothing is beyond me! I do not see how they can live in India and wear the clothes they do. The women have long, broad, thick gowns made by the Tibetan tailors. They have no style, no shape. A broad ribbon or string will be tied around the waist over the gown, and they also tie a thick quilt piece around the waist to keep the hips warm. In India! They seem to think they are still in Tibet. Their shoes we can see on them for 24 hours. I was surprised to see them sleeping with their shoes on in the night also. The shoes are not cleaned, so they stink like dead bodies. If they take off shoes and put behind door of house, I cannot go in. Sometimes shoes are so worn out they only have the upper part. They put paper in soles and continue to wear them—even to bed.

"The women use brassieres for fashion. I have seen mothers walking into the creches before other men with skirt and brassiere, with no blouse. I could not stand the sight of that, but it never bothers them. They never notice the thick dirt and stains on their dresses. One must have tremendous strength to wash those heavy gowns. A gown needs five to eight yards of cloth, plus the padding. Of course, they wash their clothes at a stream by beating on stones, but it is a very heavy job to do. They never wear flowers in their hair like Indians, but tie the colored ribbons. The women cut their hair short and bangs are very common among the young girls.

"The men have long coats and trousers. They too are made with heavy materials. They wear funny hats made in Tibet. They have long hair which they plait and tie with bright ribbons, and they put on a hat while these plaits fall on their chest in front. Most of the men wear the jackets of women and skirts which come for these refugees from Western countries." Alice giggled. "I have even seen a man wearing a brassiere under his coat. When I asked him why, he said, 'I want to keep my purse in it!'

"The men never shave their faces, and one can see the irregular whiskers and beard. Women who have hair on their faces will have hard time to get husbands. They are looked down on among the Tibetans."

"What do the children wear?"

"They also wear thick dresses of any style in summer and winter. They never like to sit on floor, but on a chair or cot. The boys will have an opening in their trousers to pass urine and it will not be closed with buttons, or zip. When they sit down, everything is exposed and dirt can get in easily. Children up to six wear trousers with these openings. The children are very fond of bright-colored clothes. They are very particular about their funny hats and caps. Even when they play in the creche building or at home, they hold their hats on tightly so they should not fall down."

"Do the women like your sari?" I asked.

"Not enough to copy it. They'd never feel at home in it."

"What about their worship? They're all Buddhists, aren't they?"

"Yes, they do worship Buddha, but I see that they do not follow all that Buddha teaches in his sacred books. Every follower of

Buddha knows that he should not kill any small creature. These people kill cows, pigs, chickens, sheep, and goats to eat, but they never kill the head lice, snakes, cobras, rats, etc. Killing these will lead them into hell, or else Buddha will create them as cobras or snakes in the next creation. They place the picture of Buddha or an image of him in the hall, along with picture of the Dalai Lama, and worship their pictures daily with regular puja. They say very strongly that Dalai Lama is God to them; he is not human, but God who has been born by incarnation. They worship evil spirits. There is no singing nor reading of holy books in their worship except repeating some words, which sounds like grumbling. They are very particular of their prayer flags in front of each family house. These prayer flags keeps the devils away from their homes.

"Men and women use prayer wheels and beads for their prayers. The same words will be repeated a thousand million times as they count their beads. They will be praying and counting the beads even when they are fighting! Their prayers are written on black wooden pieces and books. They wrap these sacred things in yellow cloth. Yellow color is the most holy color to them."

"How about their occupations? Are there any artists among them? Do they know how to carve and make things like the Indians do?"

"Their occupations are varied. We see farmers, carpenters, smithery (both black and gold), cobblers, tailors, painters, and knitters and rug makers among these people. They take great interest in ploughing and raising the crops. They love to spend their time in fields from morning until evening—with their tea kettles. The carpenters do the woodwork well, but they know only a few patterns and those which suit Tibet country. The goldsmiths do very lovely work in gold and silver, especially silver. Their spoons and rings are liked by many in India and foreign countries. The cobblers know how to make shoes of Tibet country patterns, but not ours. The tailors can stitch the clothes of their country people but not for us. They paint with bright colors. They are very fond of bright colors like deep yellow, maroon, red and black."

I drank my tea, thankful it wasn't filled with yak butter and salt. "I feel sorry for them, being so far from their own land, and still trying to remain Tibetans in India. What do they do for social life?"

"Oh, they have it all right. These people are in a different world with their social lives. Drinking is very common among them. Men and women have very close relationship. Though they are not from same family, they move very freely with any Tibetan man or woman. No privacy for them at any time. I have seen them making love in fields in daytime—men and women who are not husbands and wives. They have marriages, but use a ring, no Thali (marriage necklace of India) and no bangles (bracelets) as marriage significance. The man and the woman will sit with big Lama and a few leaders and say some prayer and drink the 'chung' (liquor), and eat heavy meat for three days. That is all for the marriage. A woman can have four or five husbands from her own country. The man can leave first wife and can have second or third at same time. They never think that these things are serious. Young girls often give birth before they marry, but take it as proud event. Such girls will never be looked down on as in India.

"Smoking is common with both sexes. Dancing is very common. They do their folk dances very well. These dances are welcomed by the Indian public even in cities. They forget themselves with heavy drinking and dancing during their festivals. Their big festival comes in the month of March (their New Year's Day) and they celebrate for eight to fifteen days. They wear jewelry, grand clothes, drink, and dance until they are half dead. They love picture-going (movies). They sing a lot but with same tune.

"They are very fond of drum dances, with funny faces made and colored in Tibetan style."

"Well, Alice, I know that you are mostly concerned with their health situation since that is your job. Are they healthy, even with their heavy clothes and wormy meat and drinking all the time?"

"No, Ammah. Their diseases are common to village people in India. Intestinal worms are very common, especially tapeworms due to lack of boiling of their pork and beef. One Tibetan passed in his stool a 20-foot-long tapeworm in the month of August while I was in bed with a bad rash! I was too sick to doctor him."

"If I'd been his nurse, I'd have been glad to be sick at that time!"

"They also have bad skin diseases due to lack of cleanliness and malnutrition. Anemia is also common because of food problems. They eat very little vegetables and fruits so they lack blood in their systems. Stomach upsets are very common due to overeating. Children even at the age of five and six years still suck the breast and live on that mother's milk.

"They are very much afraid of evil spirits and do a lot of puja when sickness is in the homes. They believe more in 'Big Lama' words than in doctors and medicine and advice during sickness. Very seldom when sick do they stick to medicine and diet. They won't rest and they won't be quiet when there is a sick patient in the home. They are very unusual people, really, Ammah." She ticked off on her fingers, "Here are some of the most unusual things about them: First, no baths are ever seen among these people. They never have a bath. They never wash their local parts after defecation."

"Good night! How can you stand their smell?"

"Well, it's pretty bad. We see beating of clothes on stones with heavy sticks to wash and clean. We see men with women's garments and women with men's garments. It doesn't matter to them which. Women carry heavy loads more then men. Men deliver babies to their own wives. They are not trained. Men are seen with two long plaits of hair tied with bright ribbons. And the majority of husbands are younger than their wives.

"Those Tibetan people are not happy people except when they are in the midst of merrymaking, and then they sit with grinning expression. They don't like to share things with others; they have a lack of a giving spirit. Fighting, gossiping are very common. They lack spirit of gratitude. They very seldom help the sick, and they give no notice at all for their neighbor. even when there is a death in the house next door. They really need a lot of time to learn manners. Honesty should be taught to them. Courtesy is not practiced among them at all. They don't care for anybody unless he is a very big person. I did my best for those people for the last 22 months. I tried to show how a Christian should live, Ammah, but it seemed of little use. One must sacrifice herself a long time to work with these people. God gave me enough love and strength to serve them, though I lost forty pounds in my weight."

"I knew you had lost a lot." I looked her over; she looked younger, and if possible, more vivacious than ever. "You look great, Alice, and it's wonderful to be with you again. As usual, you've taught me a lot today."

I felt very sad to say good-bye to Alice again. I felt as close to her as I would my sister. I had brought two beautiful sweaters for her, but the present she had brought me astonished me. It was a gorgeous black net sari, laced closely with bits of silver. It's a real heirloom piece. She told me that she'd had offers from the movie-making people in India to buy it, but all this time she was saving it for me. It originally came from Arabia; she had inherited it from her sister who was drowned in a shipwreck a few years ago. She said she'd never think of giving it to anyone else. I prize it highly.

23

My House by the Bo Tree

I was most excited to be going back to Belgaum. About an hour before the Belgaum station, if one goes by train from Bombay, he arrives at a station called Ghataprabha. We have visited in that area all our missionary career, because for quite a few years J. T. was the District Superintendent of all the Christian work there. So everyone knows us. We were shaking with excitement when the train pulled into Ghataprabha, for we knew there'd be a delegation to meet us. Delegation? The whole platform was full of people: preachers, teachers, hostel children, women, villagers, and cart drivers. When J. T. saw the great crowd, he got out his camera to take their picture—or thought he did. When he stepped off the train, he found he had gotten out his electric razor instead! Everybody burst out laughing—they knew J. T. Sahib hadn't changed a bit!

After six years in America, when I walked again into our old Belgaum house, I stood in the vast living room and cried for joy. The family of one of our Indian district superintendents lives there and has kept up the house well.

As I walked slowly all over the house, many memories came rushing toward me from every room and every corner: memories of our four lovely daughters in all their growing up years in this house; all of the children riding tricycles around the four great pillars in the living room (the house used to be a courthouse); our Indian friends coming to dinners and parties there; the time when our little Sandy almost died from malaria; memories of my killing small deadly kraits (snakes) with my shoes; the heavy rains; the mold; the room where the fairies had lived for the children; the place where our piano sat, and J. T. there playing and singing love songs to me; the love and laughter. . . . It was all there, and it almost overwhelmed me.

The next day it was so natural to go to church with my old ayah (servant who helped me with the children) to listen to J. T. in the pulpit preaching a sermon in the beautiful Kanarese language. I was astonished at how much I understood, even after so long. Jothi, my ayah, shared her Kanarese hymn book with me, and I could still read it and sing the hymns. All around me were colorful saris, and sweet little children with their hair tied in ribbons. The Belgaum people looked so clean and quite prosperous, many of them owning their own cars now.

My ayah was pathetically glad to see me. Since we had left India she had lost both her husband and her beautiful daughter who played with my Sheila all their childhood. Both had died of tuberculosis. After we left, jobs were difficult to find; they didn't have enough to eat, so could not fight the disease. Jothi was more shrunken, grayer, and lived in a little two-room house, with our family pictures scattered all over the walls and tables. She has only her two sons left now.

While in the Belgaum area we visited many of the villages we used to visit years ago. In every place, they smothered us with garlands of flowers as welcome. They had the village band to meet us and escort us, walking, into the villages. We had really come home.

In the village of Bailur we had a big celebration where I cut the ribbon to open a brand-new village church; we also had a dedication for a new village well. Several years ago, this village had no water, and people had to walk for miles just to get a little. One church in Tennessee had heard about the village through our missionary message. The young people in the church had saved money to buy a new movie projector for the church, but when they heard of Bailur's need they gave us all the money to send out to help them dig a well. That day we dedicated it.

We also dedicated other churches which Father Seamands had designed and built. In one village the pastor asked us to come over to his home, and once we arrived asked me to sit in the house, while he took J. T. to another place out the back. Attached to the house was a newly built latrine, and they asked J. T. to dedicate that! (Most village people don't have any kind of latrine, they simply use the fields!) J. T. said there was a long line of men waiting to use it as soon as it was dedicated!

It was good to be in India again! One reason for going in the month of November was so that we would be able to attend the Dharur jungle camp meeting. This camp draws about ten thousand people every year. It was like the one we used to have in Belgaum, but much larger. We also wanted Gene Moore to get a real taste of this kind of life. He did.

The meetings were held in a huge pandal—just a tent roof, but no sides. At night, this was where many hundreds of people slept also. It was very cold there at night, because it was in the middle of the jungle and by a river. Many women had on only a sari; some children were covered by a towel. One night they all got so cold at 2 A.M. that they woke up and began pounding the drums and singing. Not much sleep then! I wore a coat and a sweater, had my legs wrapped in a towel and was just comfortable. The Indian men there who had been to America all had on overcoats, and men who normally would not wear turbans had towels or shawls wrapped around their heads against the chill.

The worst part of traveling on a train in India or going to a

place like the camp meeting was the toilet situation. The trains
have only a hole in the floor. At the camp, there had been a small
mat shelter put up for the Americans. Inside a trench had been
dug, and across the trench were two small bridges of green bamboo,
put together with ropes. There were two openings, one for men
and one for women. But between the two sides was only a one-ply
mat, so it was a little disconcerting to be in there and have a man
come in the other side. It was more than disconcerting—it was
fearful to stand on those slippery bamboo footings over that awful
trench!

One night we were awakened at 2 A.M. with a voice as loud as if
it had been through a megaphone, quoting scripture and singing.
We turned over under all our covers and wondered why he didn't
get quiet and go back to sleep. He didn't. He switched from scripture to a sermon, and shouted through one point after another.
After covering my head with a pillow, stuffing kleenex into my
ears, and burying myself under the covers, and still able to hear,
I asked J. T. please to get up and go tell that man to shut up. I
just couldn't understand the mentality of anybody who could go
on for an hour and a half at that time of night. J. T. went out and
came back laughing so hard he was holding his stomach. "You just
won't believe it," he said. "That guy is about twelve feet up in the
fork of a tree, preaching."

"What in the world for?" I asked.

"Probably because he never gets any other chance to preach."

Whatever the cause, he finally ran down after about a two-and-
a-half-hour sermon. We were all sleepy the next day. Occurrences
like that just proved to us we were back in India.

Now we are back at home, and I still miss India. So do our
children. Our oldest, Sylvia, is now a doctor, a resident in Vander-
bilt Hospital in Nashville, Tennessee. Sheila has just graduated
from Asbury College, and is taking master's work in English at
the University of Kentucky. Sandy, now sixteen, is looking forward

to college in another year. Linda, now ten, says she too is going to be a doctor. Perhaps some will go back to India to be of service there.

I miss India. I miss our cook and ayah, our lovely garden, our moldy old house, the rats, cats, bats, and even the snakes. I miss our hostel boys. I miss Alice and the village preachers and teachers with whom we worked for so long. I miss my friend, the Rani of Sawantwadi. I even miss our old jeep.

But J. T. still loves me, glory still hangs low, and we still hear those angels singing. I wish I had a bo tree sprout. I'd plant it here in Wilmore, Kentucky, and really feel at home. I'd sit beside it and contemplate. Perhaps I'd be enlightened.

THE END

A sonnet for India

THE SEARCH

The fearful goddess sits on eb'ny throne.
She cares not for the cow'ring man who kneels,
Nor for the hunger nor the pain he feels.
A flashing sword, and ram's blood colors stone.
The Ganges flows along its muddy way.
A weary pilgrim prays and splashes in,
He's sure the turbid water washes sin,
But Ganges cannot cleanse his guilt away.
The fire burns hot, and 'round its dancing flame
A priest with needles dances too. His face
Is scarred with sores because his soul seeks grace.
He's not redeemed; his burden's still the same.
      My Christ is living, yes, to hear and see;
      My hungry soul cries out, He answers me.

RUTH SEAMANDS